sona
BOOKS

CAT NO: SON0554

Photography courtesy of
Getty images:

- AFP
- Bob Thomas Sports Photography
- Bongarts
- Corbis Sport
- Formula 1
- Gamma-Keystone
- Hulton Archive
- Intercontinentale/AFP
- James Moy Photography

- Moviepix
- National Motor Museum/Heritage Images
- NurPhoto
- Popperfoto
- The Asahi Shimbun
- The Klemantaski Collection
- ullstein bild
- Universal Images Group Editorial

Alamy:
- Sipa US

Editor: Martin Corteel
Proof reader: Juliette O'Neill
Contributors: Scott Reeves, Natalie Denton, Rob Clark, Steve Jenkins,
Charles Ginger, David Smith and Jamie Frier

Cover image: Getty Images

Photographs: All copyrights and trademarks are recognised and respected

Made in EU.

ISBN: 978-1-915343-14-7

FORMULA
ONE

L E G E N D S

sona
BOOKS

CONTENTS

John Player
John Player Special
John Player Special
DeLonghi
12
elf

INTRODUCTION

Over its more than 70-year history, Formula 1 has grown to become one of the most-exciting and most-watched sports in the world. While its thrilling mix of danger and drama – not to mention high speed and supreme skill – continue to keep fans entertained and engrossed, it's the characters, personalities and the rivalries of the men behind the steering wheels that are Formula 1's real star attractions. In *Formula One Legends*, some of the greatest drivers in F1 history are celebrated, from the early superstars such as Juan Manuel Fangio and Jim Clark to the golden-age greats such as Alain Prost, Ayrton Senna and Nigel Mansell to the modern masters Lewis Hamilton and Max Verstappen. The book also relives 10 of the greatest F1 races of all time; runs down the most iconic circuits; and looks at the most successful F1 teams and a selection of the sport's pioneering team bosses. So strap in and prepare to celebrate the fastest show on Earth.

LEGENDS
OF FORMULA ONE

Meet the greatest drivers who have taken to the track at the wheel of a Formula One race car

As the pinnacle of world motorsport, Formula 1 has seen many iconic drivers pass through its ranks through the years. More than 100 have passed the chequered flag to win at least one race. Thirty-four have won the Drivers' Championship. Exactly half of those – 17 – have won it more than once.

But success on the track alone doesn't guarantee that a driver will be remembered years later as a legend of the sport. To truly stand out from the pack of world champions and multiple world champions, a driver needs to display something extraordinary. Some legends are known for their sublime skill behind the wheel. Others faced up to difficult challenges with bravery. Some used their charisma to become fan-favourites, cheered onto the top step of the podium around the world. An unlucky few are remembered not only for how they drove around the track, but how they tragically died on it too. From early pioneers like Alberto Ascari and Juan Manuel Fangio, to serial winners like Michael Schumacher and Alain Prost, and not forgetting modern-day greats like Lewis Hamilton and Max Verstappen, these are the names that are forever etched in F1 folklore.

FERNANDO ALONSO
F1'S KING OF CONTROVERSY

An unswerving will to win has seen Fernando Alonso's long F1 career hit the highest of highs and lowest of lows

You don't win two F1 world titles without talent, and Fernando Alonso certainly has that in abundance. But there are so many more subtle – and not so subtle – nuances that take him to another level. Aggressive, uncompromising, a fighter and having a laser-like focus on winning are reasons enough for his success. But he also brings consistency, intelligence, adaptability and, some might say, petulance, to his driving game.

However, the true measure of this exceptional man comes from his F1 peers, who simply describe him as the closest they have seen to the complete racing driver.

Born on 29 July 1981, in Oviedo, northern Spain, his father was a keen amateur kart racer who shared his passion with his children. It wasn't long before three-year-old Alonso was jumping into a hand-built F1 lookalike pedal cart. The seeds had been sown and shortly after his seventh birthday, he entered his first proper kart race and won. He continued to rise through the karting ranks and by the time he reached his mid-teens he had a karting world championship under his belt. He knew he was good and wanted more.

In 1999, aged just 18, he got his first go in a Formula 1 car at a test session at the Circuito de Jerez, part of a deal for winning a Spanish-based single-seater championship.

After this, he knew exactly where he wanted to be – Formula 1, but he also knew he would have to be patient. But he didn't have to wait long. The beginning of the new millennium saw his career shift towards his ultimate goal. Alonso got a drive with a Minardi-backed F3000 team, but more importantly a testing contract with Minardi's F1 team. He could sense that a place in Formula 1 wasn't far away and he was right. He got his chance the following season as he was promoted to the Minardi F1 team for 2001.

WHERE IT ALL STARTED

Paired with the more experienced Tarso Marques, Alonso showed exactly what he was all about. In his first F1 outing with a back-of-the-grid race team and an uncompetitive car, he managed to outqualify Gastón Mazzacane in the Prost and Luciano Burti in the Jaguar. But, more importantly, he outqualified his new teammate by a very impressive 2.6 seconds. Alonso had shown his pedigree and though he didn't realise it at the time, he had set a pattern for the rest of the season. In the very next race

❯❯ Alonso celebrates his first world title in 2005 after grabbing third place in Brazil

INFO

Nationality
Spanish

Teams
Minardi (2001), Renault (2003-2006),
McLaren (2007), Renault (2008-2009),
Ferrari (2010-2014), McLaren (2015-2018),
Alpine (2021-2022), Aston Martin (2023-present)

Championships
2 (2005, 2006)

Number of races
355

Number of race wins
32

Number of podiums
98

Pole positions
22

INFORMATION CORRECT AS OF FEBRUARY 2023

in Malaysia he was outpaced in qualifying by his more experienced teammate, but showed him a clean pair of heels in the race itself as he once again finished ahead of Marques. An unreliable car saw successive DNFs, but when the two teammates did manage a finish, it was typically Alonso who was grabbing the glory by finishing in front. A change of driver saw Alex Yoong take over from Marques, but this did little to change the fortunes of Minardi or displace the undoubtedly talented Alonso, who was showing his worth, once again outpacing his teammate and grabbing an impressive 11th-place finish in his last race for Minardi in Japan.

THE GLORY YEARS

After just one season of racing with Minardi, Alonso turned down multiple offers of a seat with similar back-of-the-grid teams. So he was out in the cold with no seat for 2002. But Benetton boss Flavio Briatore – who was in charge of Alonso's career – was keen to get him into his Renault team to replace Jenson Button. While the tempting proposition of an F1 drive never materialised, Alonso did join Renault as a test driver. It's here that he got in over 1,640 laps in test sessions in Spain and England to hone his race skills, work with the Renault engineering team to improve his all-round

⌃ Away from Formula 1, Alonso and his Toyota teammates celebrate a second victory at Le Mans

PROTESTS, BLACKMAIL AND FINES

Fernando Alonso is not a man to avoid controversy, as demonstrated by the blocking of his teammate during qualifying for the 2007 Hungarian Grand Prix. Lewis Hamilton was meant to let Alonso pass on the track but decided not to, so he took matters into his own hands with unsubtle time-wasting behaviour as the two stacked in the pits. Hamilton didn't get back out for a second qualifying lap, meaning Alonso took pole. But not for long. After a protest from Hamilton's team, Alonso was handed a five-place grid penalty.

Alonso was not a happy man and this led to perhaps the biggest controversy of his career. The next morning, a few hours before the race, Alonso demanded a meeting with team boss Ron Dennis to 'discuss' the previous day's proceedings. Alonso threatened Dennis that if the team did not do what he wanted, he would reveal to the FIA emails he had that were relevant to the 'spygate' case. This is where chief designer Mike Coughlan was found in possession of a 780-page document of Ferrari intellectual property. Alonso insisted that McLaren make Hamilton run out

of fuel in the race. Dennis and his second in command, Martin Whitmarsh, didn't like being blackmailed and phoned FIA president Max Mosley. It is believed that it was this phone call that led to McLaren being excluded from the Constructors' Championship, receiving a $100 million fine and Alonso negotiating his way out of his contract.

» Alonso teamed up with Hamilton for a single, tension-filled season at McLaren in 2007

⬆ Alonso's Ferrari and rival Hamilton's McLaren crash out at the first corner at the start of the 2012 Belgian Grand Prix

racing knowledge, and get ready for the next season. Again, he was linked with a host of teams for 2003, but Briatore was no fool and promoted him alongside Jarno Trulli. In his first race he once again showed how good he was by outqualifying his teammate and grabbing a couple of points in the race. But the second race of the season in Malaysia is where fans really got to see what a talent Alonso was. He grabbed his first pole position and went on to get his first podium with a third-place finish. He was starting to show his true mettle and it wasn't long before he got his first F1 win in Hungary, neatly coupled with a pole position.

The 2004 season was another learning experience – and step towards glory – as during offseason Alonso got involved with his engineers and the development of the latest car, the R24. His goal for the season was a simple one – improvement. He managed a pole position, four podiums and fourth place in the championship.

Alonso's momentum was building and with a car capable of taking him to the title, he was one of the preseason favourites for 2005 and he duly delivered. He got off to a blistering start with four wins, a second, a third and the only time he was off the podium was a lowly fourth at Monaco. Two DNFs put a dent in his championship hopes but he was soon back to winning ways with victories in France and Germany, and a succession of second and thirds were topped off with victory in the final race of the season in China. Alonso had done it; he was the youngest – at the time – Formula 1 world champion at the tender age of 24 years and 58 days.

With one world championship in the bag, Alonso was keen to add another and the 2006 season saw him start as one of the favourites yet again. If 2005 saw him get off to a blistering start, the beginning of the 2006 season was stratospheric. He wasn't out of the top two in the first nine races, winning six of them. A midseason wobble saw a couple of DNFs and fifth places, but Alonso brought it home in the last three races with a victory and two second places. Alonso was once again top of the pile, but this time he was the youngest two-time world champion at 25 years and 85 days.

NEVER FELT AT HOME

Alonso had agreed to join McLaren back in 2005 and arrived as a two-time and reigning world champion looking to add a third successive title in 2007. McLaren had a competitive car, but Alonso was soon to discover that he

« Alonso celebrates becoming two-time world champion at the 2006 Brazilian Grand Prix

had a competitive teammate in the shape of rookie Lewis Hamilton. The signs for the season were there from the off as Hamilton pulled a bold move around the outside of Alonso to get ahead of his teammate on the first lap of the first race of the new season.

Race by race the tension between Alonso, Hamilton and the team slowly started to grow. Hamilton was not happy with team orders as Alonso took first place in Monaco. Two races later at the US Grand Prix, Alonso showed his frustration when he couldn't get past Hamilton. In Hungary, Alonso blocked Hamilton in the pits to ensure he couldn't do a final qualifying lap, and at Spa he forced Hamilton off the track.

But it wasn't just on the track where the tensions were rising. Off the track, Alonso's relationship with McLaren boss Ron Dennis was at an all-time low, with Dennis revealing that they were not on speaking terms. At the end of the season, Alonso missed out on winning his third title by a single point to Kimi Räikkönen, and made it quite clear what he thought: "It is not a secret that I never really felt at home." Then, almost inevitably, McLaren announced that Alonso would be leaving and returning to his former team, Renault.

⌄ After taking pole position, Alonso went on to grab his sixth win of his 2006 title-winning season at the Canadian Grand Prix

RETURN OF THE PRODIGAL SON

Alonso's short-lived reign at McLaren meant he was unexpectedly looking for a new seat for the upcoming 2008 season. He flirted with moving to Red Bull, but Benetton boss Briatore stepped into the ring with an offer that Alonso couldn't resist, and he was back with the team that brought him two world titles. But unlike previous seasons, he wasn't one of the favourites for the title. A steady rather than spectacular season saw him grab a couple of wins, a podium finish and fifth in the championship – a distant 37 points behind his old teammate Hamilton.

After declining tempting offers from Red Bull and Honda, Alonso signed a new contract with Renault, but an uncompetitive car led to a poor season by his standards with no wins, no podiums and a lowly ninth in the championship.

CLOSE, BUT NO CIGAR

Alonso was desperate to get back to winning ways and saw Ferrari as the team to make that happen. But getting there wasn't simple. A verbal agreement was to see him join in 2009, but politics got in the way. By the middle of 2009 he had made an agreement to join in 2011, but after race-fixing allegations at Renault, Alonso got his move to Ferrari in 2010 at Räikkönen's expense.

He came perilously close to that elusive third world championship in his first season, only to concede to

⌃ Alonso's Alpine gets the better of Lance Stroll at the 2021 Austrian Grand Prix

Sebastian Vettel by a mere four points. His second season didn't live up to the first, with him finishing fourth in the championship. But it was all guns blazing for the 2012 season, with the title still in the balance heading into the last race of the season. A second place for Alonso and a sixth for Vettel once again led to heartache as the German grabbed the title by just three points. The 2013 season saw Vettel run away with the title and Alonso had to settle for second – again. His last season at Ferrari saw him team up with the man he originally replaced, Räikkönen, but Ferrari simply didn't have a car that could win and Alonso finished a disappointing sixth in the championship. His career at Ferrari came to an acrimonious end.

UNFINISHED BUSINESS

Alonso's first spell at McLaren had been marked with controversy and came to a bitter end. But the years had seen both McLaren team boss Dennis and Alonso mellow and mature. Dennis conceded that Alonso was one of the best, if not the best, driver in Formula 1 and wanted him back in his car. But it didn't start well. Alonso got a concussion in preseason testing and sat out the first race of the 2015 season. He then got a DNF in the second, something he was to see seven more times that season. After finishing on a pitiful 11 points, it didn't get much better in 2016. He crashed heavily in the first race and sat out the next. But a more reliable car saw Alonso get a respectable 54 points, 33 more than his teammate Button. Then in 2017 it was back

to reliability issues, with ten DNFs and Alonso threatening to leave unless Honda and McLaren could bring him a competitive car his driving talents deserved. Unfortunately they couldn't, and the inevitable finally happened.

TIME OUT

After a less than impressive second stint with McLaren, Alonso had become disillusioned with the sport, claiming it was all becoming too predictable. He decided it was time for a new adventure, stating that there were bigger challenges outside Formula 1. But what were those challenges?

The fabled Triple Crown was one mission as he tried to win the Indy 500 in 2017, 2019 and 2020, but with little success. However, the famous 24 Hours of Le Mans was a more fruitful race ground, as he won twice in 2018 and 2019 with Toyota. But other motorsports couldn't provide the challenge he was looking for and in 2020 he decided it was time to get back to his first love – Formula 1.

THIRD TIME LUCKY

At the age of 39 Alonso was back in the F1 game, he was back in the sport he loved and the lure of a third stint with his favourite F1 family (Renault) for the 2021 season was simply too hard to resist. The team were committed to Formula 1 and getting back to the top of the F1 tree with Alpine and Alonso at the wheel. But two seasons were not quite the triumphant return Alonso would have wanted. So partway through the 2022 season Alonso announced he was replacing the retiring Sebastian Vettel at Aston Martin. He still feels he deserves a seat in Formula 1, and talent doesn't just disappear – so this double world champion will always be welcome.

ALBERTO ASCARI
HIS FATHER'S SON

The first double world champion whose death was an eerie echo of his father's

 Ascari was on course to win Lancia's first Grand Prix before he crashed at Monaco; four days later he was dead

INFO

Nationality
Italian

Teams
Ferrari (1950–1954)
Maserati (1954)
Lancia (1954–1955)

Championships
2 (1952, 1953)

Number of races
32

Number of race wins
13

Number of podiums
17

Pole positions
14

Young Alberto Ascari was the biggest fan of his father – racing star Antonio who won four pre-World Championship Grand Prix in the 1920s – so it hit hard when he died in a crash at the 1925 French Grand Prix. But he didn't avoid the sport that killed his dad – Ascari was determined to follow in his footsteps. He was recruited by Enzo Ferrari in time for the first FIA World Championship in 1950.

He picked up his first race wins in 1951 before storming to victory in the 1952 Drivers' Championship by winning the last six races of the season. No driver could get past Ascari and his lucky blue helmet. He held the lead for 304 consecutive laps across five races, a record that will surely never be broken. Ascari was almost as dominant in 1953, winning five races to become the first multiple world champion, before accepting an offer to drive for Lancia. Ascari was open about his motivations – it was all about the money – but he missed almost all of 1954 while his new team prepared the cars.

There was the potential for a long and successful partnership – Ascari earned pole position and set the fastest lap in Lancia's debut Grand Prix – but things went wrong at the 1955 Monaco Grand Prix. Ascari lost control while leading the race and his car flew through the fence and into Monte Carlo harbour. The Lancia sank; Ascari bobbed to the surface.

Four days later, a largely uninjured Ascari attended a Ferrari test session at Monza. He asked to drive but the car skidded and flipped after three laps. Ascari was flung from his seat and suffered fatal injuries. Were there portents of his death? His father died on 26 July 1925; Alberto died on 26 May 1955. Both were 36 and had won 13 Grand Prix. Both had survived crashes four days before their life-ending accidents at seemingly innocuous left turns.

⬆ Ascari racing in the Alfa Romeo P2 at the 1925 Belgian Grand Prix

RUBENS BARRICHELLO
THE WINGMAN

The ultimate teammate who helped his bosses to six Constructors' Championships

Rubens Barrichello entered F1 in 1993 and spent seven years at the back of the grid. Not until he joined Ferrari in 2000 did he have a chance to mix at the front. He rewarded his new employers with a race win in his 124th Grand Prix start when he took the chequered flag at the German Grand Prix. The German fans wanted to cheer his teammate Michael Schumacher to victory, but it was one of Barrichello's few moments in the limelight – he spent much of the next six years as Schumacher's dependable wingman.

In 2002, Barrichello obeyed team orders for Schumacher to overtake him in the final few seconds of the Austrian Grand Prix. Considering it was only the sixth race of the season, Ferrari's tactics were widely condemned and the pair were booed on the podium. Schumacher returned the favour later in the year, allowing Barrichello to pip him by 0.011 seconds in the US Grand Prix, but by then Schumacher had safely secured the Drivers' Championship. Barrichello finished a distant second.

The position-swapping made no difference to the Constructors' Championship, Ferrari easily won in 2002. It was the third of five consecutive Constructors' Championships that Barrichello won during his six years with the team.

A spell with the hapless Honda team followed and the Brazilian's career seemed to be in freefall until the team were rescued by Ross Brawn. Barrichello's two race wins earned the salvaged team the Constructors' Championship – Barrichello's sixth – as his teammate Jenson Button stormed to an unexpected Drivers' title.

When he retired in 2011, Barrichello had achieved a record that Button and Schumacher did not. He ended his career with 322 starts, while his championship-winning teammates both finished on 306.

⌃ Michael Schumacher, Rubens Barrichello and Ross Brawn celebrate on the podium of the Grand Prix of Malaysia in 2000

≫ Barrichello with the Ferrari team crew following his win at Suzuka in 2003

INFO

Nationality
Brazilian

Teams
Jordan (1993–1996)
Stewart (1997–1999)
Ferrari (2000–2005)
Honda (2006–2008)
Brawn GP (2009)
Williams (2010–2011)

Championships
0

Number of races
322

Number of race wins
11

Number of podiums
68

Pole positions
14

THE TYRE WHISPERER

The 100/1 outsider who became world champion in one of F1's greatest turnarounds

The youngest Brit to have started a Grand Prix on his debut and the sport's youngest point-scorer when he finished sixth in his second race, Jenson Button's early promise went unfulfilled during his first years in F1. Easily distracted by the flashy lifestyle, Button developed a reputation as a wasted talent. "Just a lazy playboy," was the verdict of Benetton boss Flavio Briatore, who released him after one season, as did his first three teams.

Button was rescued by BAR, the team built around Jacques Villeneuve, where he outscored his illustrious teammate. Button took on the responsibilities of team leader after Villeneuve left and propelled BAR to second in the Constructors' Championship, while he himself was third in the Drivers' Championship.

BAR were bought by Honda – during the first season in Honda's colours, Button took his maiden Grand Prix victory in 2006 – but Honda chose to step away from F1 with only three weeks until the season opener in 2009. Suddenly faced with unemployment, Button's future in F1 was saved when team principal Ross Brawn led a management buyout.

And then the dream began. To the surprise of everybody, Button took the chequered flag in six of the first seven races. Although the rest of the field narrowed the gap once they understood the aerodynamic benefits of Brawn's double diffuser design, Button had built enough of a cushion. The 100/1 outsider at the start of the season had won the Drivers' Championship.

Button didn't stay when the team was bought out by Mercedes, but moved on to McLaren where he partnered with Lewis Hamilton and Fernando Alonso, finishing second in the 2011 Drivers' Championship. He retired in 2017 as a championship winner with over 300 starts. Not bad for a lazy playboy.

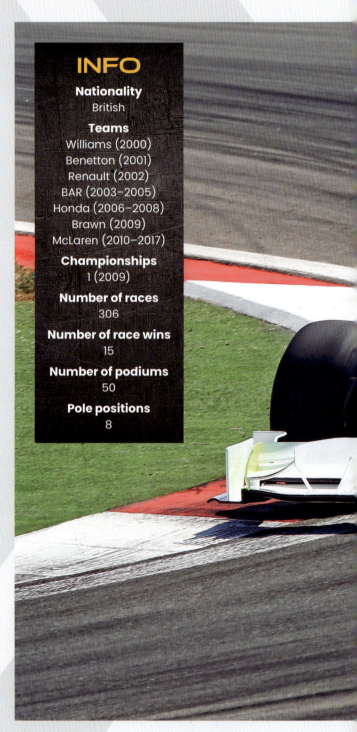

INFO

Nationality
British

Teams
Williams (2000)
Benetton (2001)
Renault (2002)
BAR (2003–2005)
Honda (2006–2008)
Brawn (2009)
McLaren (2010–2017)

Championships
1 (2009)

Number of races
306

Number of race wins
15

Number of podiums
50

Pole positions
8

> Button took a salary cut to remain with Brawn after the buyout – a decision that paid off on the track

» Button surprised many by outscoring Lewis Hamilton in 2011 to finish second in the Drivers' Championship

JIM CLARK
MR SMOOTH

The double world champion who triumphed in one of the most dominant seasons in F1 history

The danger inherent in being a Formula 1 driver was made clear to Jim Clark in only his second race. Chris Bristow and Alan Stacey were killed in separate crashes within a few minutes and a few hundred metres of each other, yet the race continued and Clark finished fifth to pick up his first Grand Prix points. Only after the race was complete were flecks of Bristow's blood spotted on Clark's car.

The following year, Clark touched wheels with the Ferrari of Wolfgang von Trips. The German's car slid up an embankment and into a fence, killing him as well as 15 spectators.

Clark held his nerve after these early tragedies to become one of the top drivers of the 1960s. He won the Drivers' Championship twice, in 1963 and 1965, on both occasions achieving the maximum score of 54 at a time when only a driver's top six scores from the ten-race season were counted. An oil leak on the last few laps of the last Grand Prix of 1964 robbed him of the opportunity to add to his titles. It was his maiden triumph in 1963 for which Clark will always be remembered, though. He won seven of ten races and only finished off the podium on one occasion. He lapped every competitor at the Dutch Grand Prix and finished the Belgian Grand Prix almost five minutes ahead of his nearest rival, despite suffering gearbox issues that meant he had to hold the lever in place when fifth gear was selected. Clark and his Lotus were simply unstoppable.

Clark was still a contender in 1968 and won the first race of the season before heading to the Hockenheimring to compete for Lotus in a Formula 2 race. Clark's car left the track after five laps – a deflating rear tyre the likely cause – and he suffered fractures to his neck and skull, dying of his injuries on the way to the hospital. At a time when fatalities were sadly common, the loss of a double world champion still shocked the motorsport world.

» As well as Formula 1, Clark also competed in sports cars, touring cars and the Indy 500

⌃ Clark was given a chance by Colin Chapman at Lotus after he finished second to his future team boss in a race at Brands Hatch

⌃ Clark racing at the 1967 Grand Prix of Mexico, in the Lotus 49 Ford Cosworth

INFO

Nationality
British

Teams
Lotus (1960–1968)

Championships
2 (1963, 1965)

Number of races
72

Number of race wins
25

Number of podiums
32

Pole positions
33

The Lotus 25 that helped Clark win the 1963 championship was stronger yet lighter than the previous models and proved dominant on the track

EL MAESTRO

The Argentinean superstar who dominated the first decade of F1 and set records that will never be beaten

Juan Manuel Fangio was a man apart from his fellow racers during the early years of F1. While most competitors were young men from privileged European backgrounds, Fangio was an Argentinean mechanic. He was just about to turn 39 and had spent years honing his skills in endurance races in his home country when the British Grand Prix kicked off the FIA World Championship in 1950.

Fangio raced for Alfa Romeo in the inaugural season and topped the points going into the final Grand Prix, but car problems forced him to retire. He attempted to get back into the race by taking over a teammate's car – the rules allowed it back then – but lasted only nine more laps before technical problems struck again and Fangio retired a second time. The following year there were no such

mishaps and Fangio won his first Drivers' Championship.

However, 1952 was a year to forget. New regulations banned Fangio's Alfa Romeo but he would have missed most of the season anyway after breaking his neck in a crash at a non-championship Grand Prix at Monza. It was an uncharacteristic error for a driver who rarely lost control and was known for winning races at the slowest possible speed.

A fit-again Fangio won four consecutive Drivers' Championships from 1954 to 1957. His win at the German Grand Prix was not just his final race win, it was one of the best. After a botched pit stop left him a minute behind the leaders, Fangio set fastest lap after fastest lap to win. The greatest driver of his era, who won nearly half of the Grand Prix he started, had left his best performance for the end.

⌃ Fangio has the highest win percentage of any F1 driver, having taken victory in 47% of the races he started

≫ Fangio in his Ferrari-Lancia D50, before winning Syracuse Grand Prix in 1956

LEGENDS OF FOR

INFO

Nationality
Argentinian

Teams
Alfa Romeo (1950–1951)
Maserati (1953–1954,
1957–1958)
Mercedes (1954–1955)
Ferrari (1956)

Championships
5 (1951, 1954,
1955, 1956, 1957)

Number of races
51

Number of race wins
24

Number of podiums
35

Pole positions
29

INFO

Nationality
British

Teams
McLaren (2007–2012), Mercedes (2013–present)

Championships
7 (2008, 2014, 2015, 2017, 2018, 2019, 2020)

Number of races
310

Number of race wins
103

Number of podiums
191

Pole positions
103

LEWIS HAMILTON

F1'S BILLION DOLLAR MAN

Unrivalled in his field, the boy who would receive a knighthood always knew he was destined for the summit of motorsport

t all started with a bold introduction. It was 3 December 1995 and Ron Dennis, multi-millionaire CEO and founder of the McLaren Group, was attending the Autosport Awards at the Grosvenor House Hotel on Park Lane in London when he felt someone tap him on the side. He turned round to be greeted by a beaming ten-year-old boy dressed in a smart suit.

"Hi. I'm Lewis Hamilton. I won the British Championship and one day I want to be racing your cars."

The boy who'd introduced himself as Lewis was clutching a booklet, which he now offered to Dennis with a polite request for his autograph and phone number, as he had done with a host of other stars that his father, Anthony, had been helping him to identify. It was a moment that Hamilton would later recall as an adult with a smile.

"My dad made this leather-bound booklet and he printed out all these pages in it, and then there was a space for the autograph, phone number and address of each individual. I remember when I was going around and saying, 'Please can you put your phone number down?' And I got phone numbers from, like, everyone at the place basically.

"So, my dad goes, 'That's Ron Dennis over there, he's the boss of McLaren that makes those cars that you love.' I knew immediately at that point, that's who Ayrton drives for and that's who I want to drive for. So, literally, before my dad had finished explaining to me about Ron Dennis, I went over to him straight away. I don't know what possessed me... where I had the confidence at the time to be able to say those things, but I guess naturally kids have lots of confidence or don't have any fear."

Impressed by his audacious yet charming new acquaintance, Dennis took the booklet and scribbled a note

inside. "Phone me in nine years, we'll sort something out then." The offer was a genuine one, but Dennis could never have dreamed that it would one day bear fruit in the form of a world championship-winning driver. First, young Hamilton would have to prove himself on the track, a journey he embarked on in 1993, racing in karting competitions.

NEW KID ON THE GRID

Born in Stevenage in Hertfordshire, England, on 7 January 1985 to Anthony Hamilton and Carmen Larbalestier, Hamilton's first taste of racing came when his father bought him a radio-controlled car. Taking to racing instantly, Hamilton proved a skilled competitor, and the following year he bested adult rivals to finish second in the national BRCA Championship. Surprised by how rapidly his son had adapted to the rigours of racing, Anthony wondered if Lewis would prove equally adept at racing a full-size motor car.

At six years old, Hamilton received a go-kart for Christmas along with a promise that would transform his life. His father vowed that, provided he continued to apply himself at school, he would support his racing career in any way he could. At times this saw Anthony juggling up to four jobs in order to pay the bills and fund his son's fledgling career.

By 1993, eight-year-old Hamilton was ready to test himself against his fellow go-karters. Any concerns about how he'd fare on the tarmac quickly dissipated as Hamilton racked up numerous wins, victories that in turn led to cadet championship titles. Yet these remarkable achievements were eclipsed in 1995 when Hamilton became the youngest winner of the British Karting Championship. Further glory arrived in 1996 as Hamilton raced to victory in the Champions of the Future series (a crown he would successfully defend in 1997). He also managed to fend off rivals to become Five Nations and Sky TV KartMasters champion. Hamilton had overcome racist taunts from fellow racers and ferocious competition on the tracks to establish himself as a major

« Lewis Hamilton celebrates on the podium during the F1 Grand Prix of Russia September 26, 2021

talent in the world of motorsport, and his upward trajectory had not gone unnoticed.

TORQUE OF THE TOWN

Such was Hamilton's meteoric rise that some punters in the know were happy to place bets on the promising young driver (12 at the time) winning a world championship before turning 25. Yet more importantly than the whisperings and knowing nods occurring in betting shops was the fact that a key player in the industry had also been observing Hamilton's efforts from afar: Ron Dennis.

In 1998, just three years after first encountering him on that fateful night in London, Dennis decided to beat Hamilton to the punch and call him, and he wasn't just ringing to congratulate him on his glittering racing career. He was calling with a life-changing offer: a place in the McLaren development programme. The Hamilton family gladly accepted.

The youngest driver to receive a contract that would lead to competing in F1, Hamilton now had the backing of one of the biggest names in racing. He instantly repaid Dennis's faith (not to mention the sacrifices of his father) by progressing up the ranks and carving out further victories at Intercontinental A, Formula A and Formula Super A level. While racing in the latter two, Hamilton would meet Nico Rosberg for the first time, a German-Finnish teammate who would one day fight him for the ultimate prize.

World and European titles further cemented his place as a rising star (a status the British Racing Driver's Club officially recognised in 2000), but arguably the most exciting chapter in Hamilton's journey to date came in 2001, when he competed in a one-off go-kart race that featured a special guest: four-time world champion Michael Schumacher. Finishing a mere four places behind the German, Hamilton earned the highest of praise from the only other man to win seven world titles: "He's a quality driver, very strong and only 16. If he keeps this up I'm sure he will reach F1." By 2007, at just 22, Hamilton would fulfil Schumacher's prophecy after spells in Formula 3 and GP2.

KING OF THE WORLD

As the 2007 season loomed, McLaren found themselves with a vacancy. Colombian Juan Pablo Montoya's decision to head to America to compete in NASCAR, combined with Finnish racer Kimi Räikkönen's transfer to Ferrari (with whom he'd win the 2007 world championship) left McLaren in need of a partner for two-time champion Fernando Alonso. After some deliberation, McLaren informed Hamilton that he would be the team's new driver.

"We reviewed the whole grid, and when we looked at the drivers other than the top three, there was no one that really shone," said Dennis. "Lewis has been in the family for a long time and he deserves the opportunity we're giving him." It would prove to be a chance that the young talent would eagerly grab with both gloved hands.

As unfazed as the boy who had stormed the world of karting over a decade before, Hamilton wasted no time in making an impression as he surged to a third-place finish to snatch a spot on the podium in his debut race at the Australian Grand Prix. Incredibly, he'd repeat the feat nine times in a row in a record-breaking rookie season, a string of astonishing finishes that included victories in Canada and the US (the first time a British driver had won a grand prix in the States since 1983). The youngest driver to ever sit at the summit of a world championship, Hamilton was flourishing at the highest level of motorsport, and while his bid for immortality was ultimately derailed by a puncture in Turkey and the snare of a gravel trap in China, finishing one point behind eventual champion Räikkönen was an unbelievable achievement and a portent of things to come.

Hamilton is widely regarded as one of the most talented drivers ever to grace a track, but behind his supreme ability lies an endless dedication to improving his craft and a

« Dennis (right) was instrumental in giving Hamilton a seat in Formula 1

level of consistency that few others can hope to match. Yet bizarrely his maiden world championship title in 2008 would be built on flashes of brilliance and moments of genius that punctuated an otherwise error-strewn season.

Everything started promisingly, with victory in Australia. But then a penalty in Malaysia was compounded by a crash in Canada, Hamilton careering into Räikkönen as the Finn waited at a red light. Additional misjudgements (some committed by the McLaren team) dogged Hamilton in Belgium and also Japan, as Stevenage's most famous son battled to keep his campaign from skidding off track.

The highlight of 2008 – and, according to many experts and pundits, his career to date – came on the rain-drenched track at Silverstone on an unforgettable July afternoon. Despite starting from fourth on the grid and facing horrendous conditions, Hamilton displayed his now famous mastery of the elements to annihilate the competition and take the chequered flag a full minute before Nick Heidfeld of BMW Sauber crossed the finish line. It would prove to be a crucial victory.

By the time the world of Formula 1 was gearing up for the season's climax in Brazil on 2 November, Hamilton had managed to notch up additional wins in both Germany and China to put himself top of the championship table by seven points. However, home favourite Felipe Massa lurked close behind, poised to drive Ferrari to victory and secure his place in the annals of F1 history.

In sixth place on the grid, Hamilton's task was clear: gain a single place and hold it. That is all it would take to make him the youngest – not to mention the first Black – F1 world champion, yet by the last lap he remained in sixth. Massa looked destined to take the crown. Nearing the final bend, Hamilton steeled himself for a manoeuvre that could secure glory or send him spinning into the nearest barrier. With Sebastian Vettel screaming along beside him, Hamilton lunged, overtaking Toyota's Timo Glock to pinch fifth place and the title in dramatic style. The boy who'd idolised Ayrton Senna as a child and confidently introduced himself to the head of McLaren had fulfilled his greatest dreams. The only Black man ever to compete in F1 had overcome seemingly insurmountable odds to stand unrivalled at the summit of a championship that had not been won by a fellow Brit since Damon Hill in 1996. But perhaps most importantly of all, he'd repaid his father's endless sacrifices, all those hours working numerous jobs, the countless drives to competitions and his unwavering support in the finest way possible.

Hamilton and teammate Rosberg fight it out on track at the 'Duel in the Desert' – the 2014 Bahrain Grand Prix

❯❯ Hamilton leads Sebastian Vettle during the US Grand Prix, October 2017

A TEST OF VETTEL

Given his astounding exploits in the previous two seasons, it was tempting to assume as the 2009 F1 season loomed that Hamilton would successfully defend his history-making title. In reality he never came close to repeating his 2008 triumph as his season began in the worst possible fashion.

After fighting his way up to fourth place from 18th in the opening Australian Grand Prix, Hamilton (with the knowledge of his team) permitted Toyota's Italian driver Jarno Trulli to speed past when a safety car was present on the track, an overtaking that they knew would result in a penalty for Trulli. Denying any wrongdoing to race officials, McLaren were quickly undermined by the emergence of radio communications that exposed the duplicity. For his part in the debacle Hamilton was disqualified in what he later called "the hardest week of my life" – so hard that he briefly wondered if stepping down from F1 was the gracious thing to do. Thankfully for the sport he eventually disregarded the notion, but the fact that he even considered it is testament to the toll the whole episode took on the young star.

To compound his misery, a string of poor results on the track turned an unwelcome spotlight on the condition of the MP4-24, a car that was lambasted as being "possibly the worst car McLaren has ever designed". Even a series of much-needed improvements couldn't reverse the team's fortunes, and despite wins in Hungary and Singapore, Hamilton finished a distant fifth behind eventual champion Jenson Button. To Hamilton and McLaren's frustration, finishing some way off the top would become a regular

occurrence in the following years as a new, more robust threat emerged: Sebastian Vettel.

After promising spells at BMW Sauber and Toro Rosso, Vettel had moved to Red Bull in 2009, a move that would reap remarkable rewards for both parties. The German's first season almost ended in instant triumph as he finished 11 points behind Button in the final standings, a result that evidently spurred the 22 year old to chase greater heights. For the next four seasons the Heppenheim hotshot would utterly dominate the world of F1, eclipsing Hamilton in 2010 to become the youngest-ever world champion and then maintaining an iron grip on the trophy in 2011, 2012 and 2013. It seemed as though Red Bull would rule the tarmac for years to come.

Throughout Vettel's reign at the peak of motorsport, Hamilton finished no higher than fourth, dipping back down to fifth in a 2011 season peppered with fiery clashes that saw him smash into Red Bull's Mark Webber and Sauber's Kamui Kobayashi among others. Arguably the nadir of a poor season came on 29 May in Monaco, when he responded to a brace of penalties by accusing officials of hounding him due to the colour of his skin, comments he later retracted. Hamilton would finish the season behind a teammate for the first time as Button finished second behind Vettel, 43 points ahead of Hamilton.

KEEP YOUR ENEMIES CLOSE

After a year spent struggling, 2012 witnessed some improvement as Hamilton raced to wins in Canada, Hungary, Italy and the US, but his fourth-placed finish in the final standings was overshadowed by the shocking revelation that he would be terminating his association with McLaren and moving to Mercedes in time for the 2013 season. By putting his name to a three-year deal with his new employers, Hamilton was securing a reunion with his childhood teammate Nico Rosberg, setting the stage for a gripping rivalry.

The move didn't immediately pay dividends for Mercedes, as Hamilton could only manage a solitary victory in Hungary (as well as several podium finishes), but it wouldn't be long before their newest recruit began to prove why they had spent big money to lure him away from McLaren, and both parties would be helped by a mandate issued by the F1 authorities that stipulated the use of turbo-hybrid engines.

Mastering the intricacies of this type of engine better than

PIONEER. ICON. ACTIVIST.

Although he will forever be known first and foremost for his achievements on the race track, Lewis Hamilton has an equally important role away from the world of F1 as an activist in the struggle against racism and inequality. As the only Black man to ever race at the highest level of motorsport, Hamilton unfortunately has first-hand experience of racism, something that he now works hard to combat by supporting movements such as Black Lives Matter and making his feelings known when cases of injustice surface, such as the killing of Breonna Taylor in March 2020.

As someone who also knew the harsh constraints of living in a family that struggled financially, in the summer of 2021 Hamilton founded Mission 44 (44 being the number he races under), to help children from underrepresented groups take their first steps in the world of motor racing, engineering, science, technology and maths. Injecting £20 million of his own money into the charity, Hamilton feels as though he has finally found his calling.

"Now I feel like I have a mission in life, and it's not about just winning championships and races – that's all cool – but actually being able to make an impact to help youngsters coming through."

∧ Flanked by Verstappen and Vettel, Hamilton takes the knee in support of the fight against racism

▲ A frustrated Hamilton abandons his car after suffering an engine blow out during the 2016 Malaysian Grand Prix

any rival outfit, Mercedes constructed a car that perfectly suited Hamilton's skillset, setting him up to completely dominate the 2014 season with 11 wins and a second world title. He would enjoy further success in the following season, racking up ten wins and a record-equalling 17 podium finishes to sweep to his third Drivers' Championship. However, 2016 would go the way of Rosberg, who snatched the title in the final race of the season in Abu Dhabi before stunning the world by announcing his retirement at just 31. "I have climbed my mountain, I am on the peak, so this feels right," Rosberg explained.

GLOBAL DOMINATION

In the wake of Rosberg's sudden departure, Hamilton publicly admitted that he "didn't care" who replaced him. Ultimately, he was right not to, as the arrival of Valtteri Bottas had no impact on the final outcome of the 2017 season. Nobody was stopping Hamilton, who seized another world title courtesy of nine wins, including a stellar drive in Spain in which he recovered from kissing wheels with Vettel and sliding off the track to overtake the German and hold on for victory.

Hamilton was equally untouchable in 2018 as he notched a record 408 points in a single season to retain his crown, finishing 88 clear of Vettel thanks to 11 wins and a remarkable 17 podium finishes once again. Eager to retain his services, Mercedes rewarded Hamilton with a £40-million two-year extension. The investment was promptly repaid in 2019 with a third successive title, clinched with a new record points haul of 413.

Of his 11 victories that season, Monaco was his finest, where

he had to hold off a promising young rival by the name of Max Verstappen. An exhausted Hamilton said afterwards, "I think it was the hardest race I've had... It was the biggest challenge I think I've had and I'm really grateful I was able to pull it off."

It seemed like it would take something of biblical proportions to stop Hamilton from continuing to dominate F1. In early 2020 it arrived in the form of the COVID-19 pandemic, which saw the new season postponed from March to July and eventually condensed to 17 races. No matter: Hamilton would storm to 11 wins again to secure a record-equalling seventh world title to put him level with Michael Schumacher. His most impressive victory came in Turkey as he overcame torrential rain to finish 30 seconds ahead of Bottas, a cleverly timed switch from wet tyres to intermediates propelling him to glory.

For four straight years nobody had managed to get near Hamilton. Sure, there had been drivers who occasionally threatened to pull level or force him to find a higher gear, but eventually all had faded away into Hamilton's slipstream, condemned to acquaint themselves with the rear of his car. There was no reason to expect that 2021 would be any different.

MAD MAX AND AN UPSET IN THE UAE

Beginning in Bahrain on 28 March, the 2021 season opened in familiar style as Hamilton screeched to his 96th career victory, becoming the first driver in F1 history to thereby win at least one race in each season they had competed in. Verstappen would immediately reply with victory in the Italian Grand Prix in week two, but a brace of Hamilton victories in Portugal and Spain quickly restored order. However, anyone who discounted Verstappen's chances at this point would be proved spectacularly wrong as the young Dutchman hit back again to notch victory in Monaco. F1 had a battle on its hands once more.

Over the course of the season, Hamilton and Verstappen regularly exchanged places at the top of the table, and by the final weekend of the season in December they had banked eight and nine wins respectively. The last race, set to be hosted in Abu Dhabi, would decide the winner.

Prior to the race, Verstappen had managed to secure pole position on the grid, with Hamilton just behind him in second. When the green light flashed a ferocious contest ensued, in which several cars either crashed or were forced to retire due to mechanical issues. Hamilton worked hard to hunt Verstappen down and then carve out a hefty time advantage as he muscled his way into first.

With just five of the 58 laps to go, a crash on turn 14 spelled the arrival of a safety car. Mercedes and Hamilton decided to keep the reigning world champion out on the track in order to maintain his position, but Verstappen took the opportunity to switch to softer tyres. Even so, five cars sat between him and Hamilton, who only had to try and hold on for the last few circuits to be able to clinch a record-breaking eighth championship.

Initially, race director Michael Masi stated that the five cars between the rivals could not pass the safety car and unlap themselves, maintaining the obstacle preventing Verstappen from pulling level with Hamilton. Then Masi changed his mind and announced that the five interlopers could in fact unlap themselves. This decision effectively cleared the route for Verstappen to speed towards Hamilton, who he duly managed to overtake and then hold off to secure his maiden world title amid a hail of complaints from Mercedes. "Michael this isn't right. Michael!" bellowed Toto Wolff to no avail. Victory had been snatched away, a result that would subsequently be confirmed when Mercedes' appeal against the decision was dismissed. In his typically humble way, Hamilton congratulated Verstappen in post-race interviews, while also praising the efforts of everyone on team Mercedes.

ARISE, SIR LEWIS

Losing out on an eighth world championship understandably hit Hamilton hard, and rumours circulated that the perceived injustice of Verstappen's triumph may convince Hamilton to retire, although Mercedes were quick to dismiss the idea that Hamilton wouldn't bid for the title in 2022. Yet the opening

race in Bahrain on 20 March loomed ever closer without a definitive answer. Could arguably the greatest F1 driver in history really be poised to step away from the sport that had defined his life and propelled him to greatness?

Hamilton's appearance at the launch of Mercedes' car for the 2022 season finally put an end to the rumours. While his continued presence on the track had now been assured, what had always remained beyond doubt was Hamilton's place in the history books. A fashion icon and dedicated activist off the track, he was recognised for his achievements in the 2021 New Year's Honours list with a knighthood, a title bestowed upon him by Prince Charles at Windsor Castle just three days after his defeat in Abu Dhabi.

With Hamilton returning to the cockpit in 2022, the rivalry with Verstappen could shape Formula 1 for years to come. Every champion needs a worthy adversary, and Verstappen is shaping up to fulfil that role with aplomb. Even so, if Hamilton had ultimately chosen to end his career in racing, he would have done so safe in the knowledge that he had fulfilled his wildest dreams seven times over and cemented his place alongside the legends he used to watch as a child. Yet perhaps his greatest achievement was standing by his values and sticking to a promise he made to himself. "I don't aspire to be like other drivers – I aspire to be unique in my own way," he once said. Whatever the future holds, Sir Lewis Hamilton will continue to do things his way, and there is no better path to tread than your own.

» The last race of the 2021 season went down to the wire in Abu Dhabi, with Hamilton and Verstappen battling it out on the track

INFO

Nationality
British

Teams
Lotus (1958–1959,
1967–1969)
BRM (1960–1966)
Walker (1970)
Brabham (1971–1972)
Hill (1973–1975)

Championships
2 (1962, 1968)

Number of races
176

Number of race wins
14

Number of podiums
36

Pole positions
13

GRAHAM HILL
MR MONACO

The two-time world champion and the only driver to have won the Triple Crown of Motorsport

Graham Hill didn't exactly set the world alight on his debut in Formula 1. Racing for Lotus during its first F1 campaign, Hill's first seven races ended in retirement. His two seasons with Colin Chapman saw Hill fail to win a single point, though he would return later in his career with more success.

In the meantime Hill switched to BRM, an outfit that seemed to have as poor an outlook as Lotus, but Hill put in long hours with his mechanics to help improve the cars until, in 1962, he won four races and topped the Drivers' Championship. Over the next three years he finished second, twice to Jim Clark and once to John Surtees. The loss to Surtees in 1964 was particularly hard. Hill scored 41 points to Surtees' 40, but since a driver's best six finishes only counted, Hill's total dropped to 39 while Surtees – who retired four times – stayed on 40.

Hill returned to Lotus in 1967 and teamed up with Jim Clark, but the two-time world champion was killed after one Grand Prix in 1968. Hill responded by driving the fragile and unpredictable Lotus without fear, winning three races and finishing second in three more to match his late teammate by winning a second Drivers' Championship.

Hill's time as a frontrunner came to an end a year later. When his Lotus stalled at the US Grand Prix, he got out to push-start his own car. He got going again but a tyre failure sent the car into a bank and Hill, who had not buckled his safety belt, was thrown from the car. Although he recovered from serious leg injuries and returned to F1, his six years with Walker, Brabham and his own Hill team were as unsuccessful as his first two years in the sport. His death in 1975 robbed him of the chance to see his son Damon become the first son of a world champion to also win the title.

« Hill drove a Lotus in the team's inaugural Grand Prix in the principality and returned to triumph in Monte Carlo five times

⌃ Hill overseeing his son Damon in the driving seat at the Silverstone Circuit, 27 April 1967

NIKI LAUDA
THE COMEBACK KING

Like many drivers, Niki Lauda had to buy his way into motor racing, but this three-time world champion almost paid for it with his life...

Despite having the luxury of being born into a prestigious and wealthy Austrian business dynasty (Vienna, 22 February 1949), Niki Lauda had no choice but to find his own funds to fulfil his dreams of entering the expensive world of motor racing, as his ambitions were met with unwavering disapproval from his father. After securing numerous bank loans in 1968, Lauda was able to buy his way onto the Mini team, competing in Formula Vee and Formula 3. By 1971 Lauda was eager to move on, and more importantly up, so he secured a £30,000 bank loan against his own life insurance policy in order to win a seat on Team March, racing in Formula 2, and later Formula 1.

INFO

Nationality
Austrian

Teams
March (1971–1972)
BRM (1973)
Ferrari (1974–1977)
Brabham (1978–1979)
McLaren (1982–1985)

Championships
3 (1975, 1977, 1984)

Number of races
171

Number of race wins
25

Number of podiums
54

Pole positions
24

The Austrian's F1 debut came on home soil in August 1971, at the Österreichring circuit (now the Red Bull Ring), where his car failed due to handling issues on the 20th of 54 laps. Although Lauda showed great potential, it was the only chance he had to compete at the top level that season. For the 1972 season, Lauda was a fully fledged March team driver, competing in all rounds, but at the helm of a less than mediocre car he wasn't able to make the impact he had hoped.

With no qualifications to fall back on, Lauda was determined to make it work in the world of racing, so in 1973 obtained yet another loan, this time securing a seat on the BRM team. It was here his talent began to shine, gaining the attention of Enzo Ferrari, who, after a recommendation from Lauda's former teammate Clay Regazzoni, signed him in 1974.

Things turned a corner for the Austrian once behind the wheel at Ferrari, who hadn't had a Drivers' Champion in a decade. Lauda claimed his first podium on his debut race for the Italian car manufacturer – coming second in the Argentine Grand Prix, then just three races later he claimed his first F1 victory at the Spanish GP, giving Ferrari their first win in two years. He finished fourth in the championship that year, thanks to what the media summarised as a "clinical and somewhat calculating approach to driving", earning him the moniker 'The Computer'. Lauda did little to alter this somewhat cold and unsentimental persona in the minds of racing fans, and even admitted to giving away his "ugly" and "useless" trophies in exchange for a lifetime of free car washes at his local garage. During his career Lauda was also given the nickname 'The Rat', which eventually went on to become 'Super Rat', then 'King Rat', not only due to his buck-toothed appearance, but because of his racing style, which was often described as tough, focused and tenacious.

Lauda took his first World Drivers' Championship in 1975 after some particularly gritty races, romping to victory in Monaco, Belgium, Sweden, France and the USA. After winning five races in 1976, all signs pointed to Lauda pulling in back-to-back championships, but unfortunately tragedy was waiting just around the corner.

A week before the German Grand Prix at the Nürburgring circuit, Lauda called upon his fellow competitors to boycott the race as he felt there was an overwhelming lack of safety measures in place. Most of the drivers voted against the boycott and the race went ahead. On the second lap Lauda's car, thought to have suffered rear suspension failure, veered into the track wall at full speed, where it immediately burst

Lauda raises the trophy in the air after finishing in first place to win the 1984 Grand Prix at Brands Hatch

into flames before being struck by the oncoming car of Brett Lunger. A safety marshall rushed to the scene, along with racers Harald Ertl, Guy Edwards and Arturo Merzario, who together were able to wrestle Lauda's body, shrouded in flames, from the cockpit. Hospitalised with first to third degree burns, broken bones and lung damage due to the inhalation of toxic fumes, things looked so bleak for Lauda that a priest was called in to read him his last rites. Miraculously, however, Lauda recovered and just five and a half weeks later, with blood seeping from bandages around his head, he finished fourth in the Italian GP. The fire from the accident led to severe facial scarring and disfigurement for Lauda. He also lost half of his ear and the hair on the right side of his head, as well as his eyebrows and eyelids. As such he began wearing his now iconic red baseball cap and, living up to his 'shrewd' media persona, secured a tide of highly lucrative sponsorship deals to adorn its front.

Although Lauda had missed two races while recovering from the accident (Austria and the Netherlands), he was still in contention for the 1976 championship, which came to a close in a showdown at the Japanese GP, where Lauda led his supposed racing rival – Great Britain's James Hunt – by just three points. Torrential rain swept in on race day and Lauda, among others, withdrew at the end of the second lap insisting it was too dangerous to continue. Later Lauda revealed the conditions were made worse by the fact his eyes hadn't fully healed from Nürburgring, as damage to his tear ducts caused his eyes to water excessively and he was still unable to blink effectively. The decision to withdraw, which saw Hunt

Part of Lauda's lasting legacy is the positive influence and mentorship he shared with younger racing stars, including Lewis Hamilton, who he convinced to move from McLaren to Mercedes in 2012

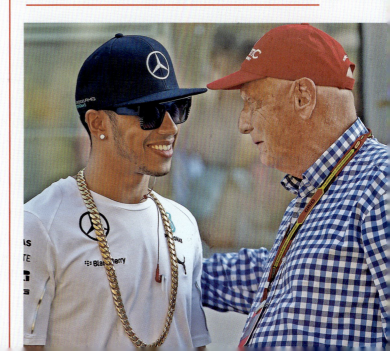

announced as the 1976 champion, divided opinion, with some hailing Lauda as brave (Hunt included), while others criticised him for being a coward, reportedly including Enzo Ferrari, who allegedly made plans to replace him.

Using the doubt of others to spur him on, Lauda seized the 1977 championship title with two races still to go. His critics denounced his success as the result of being tactical rather than using outright pace – Lauda had finished well across the board but had only managed to secure three outright wins, in South Africa, the Netherlands and Germany, which in light of Lauda's accident was held at Hockenheimring. Nevertheless, Lauda's early championship victory saw him refuse to compete in the last two races of the season and then quit Ferrari, as friction had continued to escalate with his new teammate Carlos Reutemann, who had previously been brought in to serve as Lauda's replacement.

After Ferrari, Lauda transitioned to Bernie Ecclestone's Brabham team in 1978, where, despite having to retire the problematic car in nine out of 14 races, he was able to finish fourth at the end of the season. The following year only yielded more disappointment for Lauda, with the former champ finishing 14th, as he was only able to finish two races. After coming fourth at the Italian Grand Prix at Monza (the 13th race of 15 that season) and winning the 1979 Dino Ferrari Grand Prix, a non-championship Formula 1 race held at

❯ Niki Lauda trapped inside his Ferrari, engulfed in flames after crashing into a barrier on the second lap of the German GP in 1976

Imola, Lauda walked away from motor racing claiming to be "tired of driving round in circles".

Far from 'retiring', Lauda spent the following years in the aviation industry (something he would continue to be involved in for the rest of his life), running his previously founded Lauda Air, a charter airline service, where he also served as one of its pilots. Said to be in need of more funds to expand his aviation operation, Lauda returned to Formula 1 in 1982, signing with McLaren for a record-breaking (at the time) $5 million.

Although he failed to start on pole once in 1984, McLaren's faith in the former champ was rewarded when the Austrian narrowly scraped past his much younger teammate, Alain Prost, to clinch the title by just half a point. The result came down to the last race of the season, held at the updated Estoril circuit in Portugal. Championship contender Prost held strong in first place, while Nigel Mansell chased his tail in second, and current top dog Lauda moved up from 11th place on the grid to third, but that wasn't going to be enough to beat the Frenchman in the title race. Only when Mansell's brakes failed, forcing the Brit to retire, was Lauda able to move up to the second spot, clinching his third and final championship in the process.

Although Lauda retired from racing cars at the end of the 1985 season (finishing tenth), he never truly left the world of racing. He went on to work as an adviser for Ferrari (and later Daimler AG), team principal for Jaguar, a TV commentator (he was fluent in four languages), was the author of five books, and a non-executive chairman for the Mercedes F1 team. It was here that he became a mentor and close friend

The infamous rivalry between James Hunt and Lauda was used as the basis for the film Rush

to Lewis Hamilton, and is credited with persuading the young superstar to move to the German constructors, where he has gone on to dominate the sport for the best part of a decade, winning six championships. Lauda, who became an International Motorsports Hall of Famer in 1993, even made a cameo in the 2013 movie Rush, which dramatised the 1976 championship battle between himself and Hunt.

Outwardly Lauda, who was married twice and had four children, seemed to be invincible, but he had to undergo two kidney transplants (1997 and 2005), as well as one for his lung in 2018. He returned to hospital in May 2019 for dialysis treatment on his kidneys, but passed away peacefully in his sleep on 20 May, aged 70. A moment of silence was held in his honour before the 2019 Monaco GP, where Lewis Hamilton and Sebastian Vettel donned special commemorative helmets. Numerous drivers, dignitaries and other celebrities attended his funeral in Vienna, paying their respects to one of the sport's greatest drivers of all time.

THE 1982 DRIVERS' STRIKE

Lauda was known for his tenacity in the paddock as much as he was on the track, and one of the most instrumental things the Austrian driver did off the track during his career was to safeguard the negotiating rights of drivers. This was most notable before his first race back behind the wheel in 1982. Before the opening race of the season at Kyalami, South Africa, Lauda, along with Ferrari drivers Didier Pironi and Gilles Villeneuve, organised a so-called 'drivers' strike' after refusing to sign F1's new contract that included a clause known as the 'Super Licence', which, according to Lauda and co, made it harder for drivers to negotiate their contracts. All the drivers but one backed the strike, and refused to leave the Sunnyside Park Hotel in Johannesburg until their

demands were met. Concerned the younger drivers might be swayed overnight in their individual rooms by the F1 bosses' ultimatum of 'return now, or be banned for life', Lauda had mattresses brought into the banqueting hall, where they barricaded themselves in using a grand piano, which also served as entertainment, with drivers such as Villeneuve and Elio de Angelis tinkling the ivories to keep morale high. As there was no bathroom within the hall, the drivers were trusted to leave and return, only Teo Fabi abandoned the cause, turning tail and informing Jean-Marie Balestre and Bernie Ecclestone of the group's plans, and according to Keke Rosberg, "lost all our respect forever". The next morning the drivers' demands were met and the race went ahead with Lauda taking fourth.

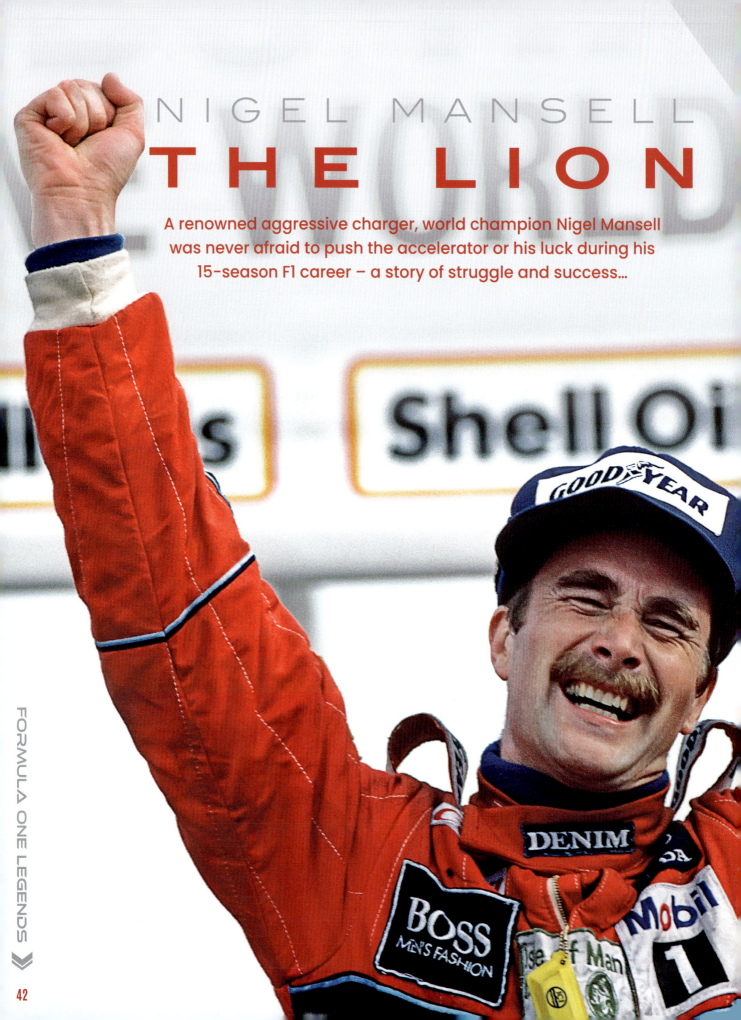

NIGEL MANSELL
THE LION

A renowned aggressive charger, world champion Nigel Mansell was never afraid to push the accelerator or his luck during his 15-season F1 career – a story of struggle and success...

Getting a taste for driving when he was seven and inspired by Scottish racer Jim Clark, Nigel Mansell (born 8 August 1953) was always drawn to the world of racing, but facing the disapproval of his father and using his own money, Mansell came to the sport a little later in life than most racers. After a stint in karting, the Brit entered the Formula Ford series in 1976, winning six of the nine races he competed in, the first of which was his debut. His talent only grew, and in 1977 he was crowned the British Formula Ford champion, despite breaking his neck in a practice session earlier that season, which according to medical staff almost saw the champion become a quadriplegic. Ignoring advice from doctors to rest for six months and not drive competitively again, Mansell returned to racing, after having quit his job as an aerospace engineer and selling the majority of his belongings to fund his passion just three weeks before the accident.

This was perhaps the world's first insight into Mansell's infamous win or bust mentality, which not only sums up the man himself, but his 'do or die' racing style.

By selling the house he and wife Roseanne owned, Mansell was able to buy his way into Formula 3 (1978-80), but a horrific collision that saw his March-Triumph cartwheel across the track, put him back in hospital, this time with a crushed vertebrae. But Mansell was determined to return to racing, and after dazzling Lotus bosses at a tryout, he became the test driver for their Formula 1 team, even though he later confessed to being full of painkillers at the test session.

Far from being happy with his lot, Mansell was desperate to prove himself and after showing his blossoming skill, not to mention setting Lotus's fastest Silverstone lap time, the constructor's owner, Colin Chapman, gifted him with three F1 races in 1980. The first of these was the Austrian Grand Prix, but engine failure on the developmental version of the Lotus 81 was to mar his debut. Not only was he forced to retire on the 40th of 54 laps, but a fuel leak in the cockpit left Mansell with first and second-degree burns on his rear. Mansell's brakes failed on his second race during the Dutch Grand Prix, and he wasn't even able to start the third after an accident during qualifying at Imola. Despite these setbacks, the plucky Brit had done enough to impress Chapman, who rewarded Mansell with Mario Andretti's seat (after he moved to Alfa Romeo) for the 1981 season. Plagued with a troublesome

« Mansell celebrates after his win at the 1986 British Grand Prix held at Brands Hatch, where one year earlier he won his first-ever Formula 1 race

INFO

Nationality
British

Teams
Lotus (1980–1984)
Williams (1985–1988, 1991–1992, 1994)
Ferrari (1989–1990)
McLaren (1995)

Championships
1 (1992)

Number of races
187

Number of race wins
31

Number of podiums
59

Pole positions
32

car that was unreliable at best, Mansell only managed to complete 24 out of 59 starts during his four years as a full-time driver with Lotus, although he did achieve five third-place finishes, with his first podium appearance at the 1981 Belgian Grand Prix, where he'd impressively jumped up seven places during the race.

In the midst of the 1982 season, Mansell, motivated by the need to earn extra money, announced his intention to compete in the 24 Hours of Le Mans race. Concerned the event was an unnecessary risk, Chapman, who had also become a close friend of the driver, personally gave Mansell the £10,000 he was offered, not to take part, and extended his contract to the end of the 1984 season, in a deal that allegedly made Mansell a millionaire. After Chapman's death in December 1982, in-team relations diminished over the following years, but where Lotus boss Peter Warr had seen obstinance, Frank Williams saw determination, offering Mansell a 1985 seat on his team alongside the 1982 champ, Keke Rosberg. Despite an okay start to the season, and a terrifying middle in which Mansell – while qualifying for the French Grand Prix – broke the record for the highest speed crash in F1 history (200mph/322km/h) resulting in a concussion that stopped him from competing the next day, the Brit would go on to repay Williams' faith. After 72 F1 starts, Mansell secured his first Formula 1 victory at the 1985 European Grand Prix held at Brands Hatch, England, and immediately followed it up with another in South Africa.

Mansell quickly established himself as a contender for the

world championship in 1986; one of his greatest seasons, racing to victory five times, and appearing on the podium nine. One of his second-place finishes was at the Spanish Grand Prix, which featured one of the closest finishes in F1 history, with just 0.014 seconds making all the difference between Mansell and Ayrton Senna. The championship came right down to the wire, with three drivers vying for the title:

⌄ Mansell, in his number 5 Williams, just inches behind Ayrton Senna's McLaren during the closing laps of the 1992 Monaco Grand Prix (a circuit he never won)

Alain Prost, Mansell and his new Williams teammate, Nelson Piquet, who publicly called the British driver an "uneducated blockhead" and criticised his wife Roseanne's appearance. Mansell only needed to finish third to win, but with just 19 laps to go, his left-rear tyre exploded on the Adelaide Street Circuit, handing Prost the second of his four championships. Things weren't all bad, however, as Mansell was voted the BBC Sports Personality of the Year (something he would later win again in 1992, being one of only four people to do so).

True to form, 1987 was another rollercoaster year for Mansell. Perhaps the highest high was an emotional victory at Silverstone, where he made up a staggering 28-second deficit to beat his rival Piquet. On the flipside, during qualifying for the penultimate race of the year (Suzuka in Japan), Mansell, attempting to beat Piquet's lap time, hit a guardrail and crashed in spectacular fashion, resulting in a spinal concussion that saw him not only miss the last two races, but allowed Piquet to scoop his third championship, calling it "a win of intelligence over stupidity", with Mansell finishing as runner-up for the second year in a row.

» Mansell tallied 187 races across 15 rollercoaster seasons, here seen praying inside the cockpit of his 1987 Williams before winning the Spanish Grand Prix

WHY MANSELL LEFT LOTUS

When Mansell's boss at Lotus and good friend Colin Chapman died suddenly in 1982, the driver was reportedly devastated, and with his champion gone, relations at the team quickly became turbulent. New team principal Peter Warr made no secret of extending preferential treatment, not to mention a better, turbo-charged car, to the team's number one driver, Elio de Angelis. The new boss even denied Mansell the brake pads he needed for his final race in Portugal, which saw him forced to retire from second place with just 18 laps to go. So it was no surprise that when the 1984 season came to a close, in which Mansell had made it into the top ten for the first time, coming joint ninth with Senna, Lotus announced they would be heading into the next season without Mansell. This, even after Mansell had wowed the world with his unparalleled grit and determination at the one-off Dallas Grand Prix, where temperatures soared above 40°C (104°F). Although leading the pack for well over half the race (after netting his first-ever F1 pole), Mansell's failing car limped to a stop on the home straight. Mansell leapt out and began pushing his Lotus towards the finish line, determined to finish. Overcome by the oppressive heat and sheer exhaustion, he collapsed just before the end in front of a cheering crowd and the world's media.

▲ Battling intense heat and exhaustion, Mansell pushed his broken-down Lotus-Renault 95T towards the finishing line of the US Grand Prix held in Dallas, collapsing just before he reached it

Where 1987 ended on a sour note, 1988 looked full of promise. Piquet had moved to Lotus and Mansell, who had racked up more wins in the previous two seasons than anyone else on the roster, was for the first time in his career a team's number one driver. However, things didn't quite go to plan, mainly because Honda took its turbo power to McLaren, which left Williams clutching at experimental straws, most of which failed to pay off. Car trouble combined with a bout of chickenpox meant Mansell was only able to compete in two out of 14 races, although somewhat miraculously, both of these resulted in podium finishes.

Mansell was seeing red in 1989 – driving for Ferrari. Said to be the last driver personally picked by Enzo Ferrari, who even gifted the Brit a 1989 Ferrari F40, Mansell was keen to please. And that he did, winning his inaugural race for the team at his least favourite track, not to mention the home circuit of his arch-rival, Piquet – Autódromo Internacional Nelson Piquet in Brazil. The race sparked a tide of adoration from Italian fans who admired Mansell's fearless, passionate approach to driving, earning him the nickname, 'il leone' (The Lion). Changes in engineering rules meant Mansell was the first-ever driver to win a race with a car that featured a semi-automatic gearbox, the gearbox that would go on to plague the rest of his season. This, plus other technical troubles, caused Mansell to retire at seven out of 16 circuits. Disqualified at the Canadian Grand Prix for reversing in the pit lane, Mansell was also banned from the following Grand Prix meet in Spain. However, in every one of the six races he did finish that year, he clinched a spot on the podium, including a win in Hungary (where he had started 12th), totalling enough championship points to cruise into fourth place.

Sadly for Mansell, 1990 rewarded him only with a bad

case of déjà vu – yet another string of engineering issues and seven retirements. Despite generating just one win (in Portugal), Mansell totalled enough points to end the season ranked fifth. Another issue had been that he was paired with reigning champ Prost, with things souring when the Brit noticed his car handled dramatically differently at Silverstone than it had in the previous race in France. After investigating the matter with the team's mechanics, Mansell discovered Prost had made the team switch their cars, believing Mansell to have the superior vehicle.

Mansell left Ferrari for his second of three stints at Williams, which was undoubtedly the most successful. Mansell was runner-up in the title race for the third time in 1991, netting a total of five wins, including the Spanish Grand Prix where he went wheel-to-wheel with Senna at 200mph and Silverstone, where he famously gave the reigning (and would-be-again) champ a lift back to the pits on his victory lap, after the Brazilian's car died on the final lap. But 1992 was the year Mansell would finally be king of the track. He enjoyed five consecutive wins straight out the gate, just missing out on the top spot in the sixth round in Monaco by 0.2 seconds. A trio of wins came midseason, including one at Silverstone,

≪ Two of Mansell's most publicised rivalries were with drivers Nelson Piquet (left) and Alain Prost (centre), pictured here with Mansell during the 1986 Austrian Grand Prix at Osterreichring

⌃ Involved in 32 crashes during his career, Mansell was no stranger to danger. Here he collided with Thierry Boutsen at the 1989 French Grand Prix

which saw him crowned as the most successful British driver of all time with his 28 wins, surpassing Jackie Stewart's record of 27. Euphoric, a wave of joyful spectators, who had endured the three-time runner-up's highs and lows right alongside him and shared the common belief that this would be Mansell's year, invaded the track in an outpouring of 'Mansell Mania', rejoicing in their hero's victory before the final lap had even finished. Once the chequered flag had waved, thousands more (this writer, aged just eight, included), joined the leagues of celebrators streaming across the circuit towards the paddock to witness the winner on the podium raise his trophy proudly in the air. Just two races later, Mansell (by then 39), not to mention his army of long-suffering yet loyal fans, were rewarded for their patience as the racer, after coming second at the Hungarian Grand Prix, finally took the title of world champion, setting the record for competing in the most races (180) before winning the F1 championship. With five races still to go, Mansell also snared the record for winning the title in the fewest races since the 16-race season was introduced, as well as most wins and poles in one season (all of which have since been broken).

Then, a falling out with Willams, largely to do with money and the fact that Prost was rumoured to be the teammate

for the 1993 season, saw Mansell announce his retirement and move to the USA, where he competed in the CART IndyCar, becoming the first-ever rookie to take pole and win his debut race. Despite a severe crash that injured his back, Mansell won the championship and is the only driver to hold both the Formula 1 and CART championships simultaneously.

The racing season in 1994 was overshadowed by the tragic death of motorsport legend Senna (who was driving for Williams) during the third race of the season at Imola. Now left with no world champions on the grid (with Prost retiring following his title win the year before) and dwindling viewing figures, F1 bosses were desperate to get Mansell back. A deal was worked out around his IndyCar commitments that allowed him to return for one midseason race at the French Grand Prix for Williams, as well as the final three races. Not in a position to compete for the championship, Mansell's main role was to boost Williams' standings in the Constructors' Championship and support his British teammate Damon Hill in his bid for the title. Hill missed out on becoming champ that year by one point to Michael Schumacher, after the two controversially clashed during the last race of the season in Australia, where Mansell went on to claim his last-ever Formula 1 win.

Subbed out for David Coulthard in 1995, Mansell moved to McLaren, where he missed the first two races due to being too wide to fit inside the narrow cockpit. Despite the team creating a new car for him in just 33 days, allowing him to compete at Imola (where a crash saw him finish tenth), Mansell felt the vehicle handled poorly. After the Spanish Grand Prix (the fourth round), he quit motorsport for good, although he had a brief dalliance with British Touring Car in 1998.

A father of three and still married to wife Roseanne, Mansell retired a rich and contented man, owning several successful business ventures, and he was inducted into the Motorsports Hall of Fame in 1995. He will forever be remembered as a hard charger with a death-or-glory driving style, who accumulated 30 fastest laps, 31 wins, 32 pole positions, but who also endured 32 spectacular crashes.

» Mansell lifting the winners trophy at the 1992 British Grand Prix

INFO

Nationality
British

Teams
HWM (1951–1952)
ERA (1952)
Connaught (1952–1953)
Cooper (1953)
Moss (1954)
Maserati
(1954, 1956–1957)
Mercedes (1955)
Vanwall (1957–1958)
Walker (1958–1961)
BRP (1959)

Championships
0

Number of races
66

Number of race wins
16

Number of podiums
24

Pole positions
16

 Moss's 16 Grand Prix victories is the most of any non-world champion driver

STIRLING MOSS
THE BRIDESMAID

A British icon and the greatest driver never to become world champion

Alfred Moss wanted his son to join the family business and become a dentist. Instead, Stirling chose to emulate his father another way. Alfred was an amateur racing driver who finished 16th in the 1924 Indianapolis 500. Stirling chose to join the ranks of Formula 1 in 1951, initially in a succession of barely competitive cars, even paying for his own Maserati and entering as a privateer. He scored points in just one race in his first four years and was still running by the chequered flag only six times out of 16 starts.

In 1955, Moss finally hit the big time. He was signed by Mercedes to partner Juan Manuel Fangio. In a season hit by tragedy – four Grand Prix were cancelled after 80 spectators were killed at the 24 Hours of Le Mans – Moss was second only to Fangio and won the British Grand Prix, his first victory, thanks in part to Fangio easing off near the chequered flag.

Little did Moss know that it would be the first of four consecutive second-place finishes in the Drivers' Championship. Three times he finished behind Fangio, while his fourth was a single-point loss to Mike Hawthorn in 1958. Hawthorn could thank Moss's sporting conduct for that particular win. When Hawthorn was threatened with disqualification at the Portuguese Grand Prix, Moss came to his defence and persuaded the stewards to allow Hawthorn's second-place finish (and six crucial points) to stand. Moss retired after three consecutive third-place finishes in the Drivers' Championship and a huge shunt at a non-championship race at Goodwood in early 1962. Moss recovered but never raced F1 again, embracing the title he was universally given – the best driver never to win the Drivers' Championship – claiming it made him more memorable than many of the men who did become world champion.

❯❯ Moss shared the driving duties with Tony Brooks for Vanwall and won the 1957 British Grand Prix, the first victory for a British constructor

NELSON PIQUET SR
THE FORGOTTEN CHAMPION

The Brazilian who drove under the radar to win three Drivers' Championships

INFO

Nationality
Brazilian

Teams
Ensign (1978)
BS Fabrications (1978)
Brabham (1978–1985)
Williams (1986–1987)
Lotus (1988–1989)
Benetton (1990–1991)

Championships
3 (1981, 1983, 1987)

Number of races
204

Number of race wins
23

Number of podiums
60

Pole positions
24

Poor Nelson Piquet. His hat-trick of Drivers' Championships should see him considered a legend, but in many people's eyes he remains 'the other guy'. He'll always be the Brazilian overshadowed by the great Ayrton Senna, while British fans mostly remember him as Nigel Mansell's teammate during two tumultuous seasons with Williams. Piquet began his F1 career in 1978, driving an Ensign for a single race before switching to BS Fabrications for the next three.

His solitary finish – ninth in Italy – was enough to convince Bernie Ecclestone to give him a seat at Brabham for the final race of the season. He remained there for the next seven years and helped steer the team from an unreliable mess in 1979 to race winners and championship contenders in 1980.

Three wins were enough to see Piquet take the Drivers' Championship in 1981 by a single point from Carlos Reutemann. After his defence ended in a disappointing 11th place in 1982, Piquet returned to the top of the table in 1983, this time two points ahead of Alain Prost.

Aware that Ecclestone wasn't paying him what he was worth, Piquet moved to Williams and reportedly trebled his salary. However, he found himself clashing with teammate Nigel Mansell. As a double world champion, Piquet thought he deserved a respect that Mansell did not show. Their infighting probably gifted the 1986 title to Prost, although Piquet made amends when he took the title in 1987 despite winning only three races to Mansell's six.

Four more seasons in F1 followed; two with Lotus and two with Benetton, where he finished an impressive third in the Drivers' Championship in 1990. In his final season, Piquet was the old hand showing the ropes to a new teammate, a rising star by the name of Michael Schumacher. Not for the first time in an illustrious career, Piquet found himself as 'the other guy'.

« Piquet's 1983 Drivers' Championship victory was the last time a Brabham driver claimed the title

INFO

Nationality
French

Teams
McLaren (1980)
Renault (1981–1983)
McLaren (1984–1989)
Ferrari (1990–1991)
Williams (1993)

Championships
4 (1985, 1986, 1989, 1993)

Number of races
199

Number of race wins
51

Number of podiums
106

Pole positions
33

ALAIN PROST
LE PROFESSEUR

In an era of outstanding talents, Alain Prost managed to set himself apart

Alain Prost attracted controversy and conflict wherever he went. He was fired by two Formula 1 teams, driven out of another, and endured a toxic working relationship with Ayrton Senna. He was forced into an involuntary year-long 'sabbatical' from the sport even after winning three world championships and setting the record for Grand Prix victories.

And yet he was a thoroughly professional, calm and often affable man. If controversy kept finding him, it was because controversy came looking, not the other way around. Of course, nobody can survive in Formula 1, let alone climb to the top of the heap, without a certain amount of ruthlessness, but Prost was known for the coolness of his driving. In a sport that famously lived on the edge, and all-too frequently strayed a little too far beyond it, Prost refused to push himself to the limit. It is remarkable to consider that he might have won even more races, and even more titles, had he pushed harder. Prost, in his pragmatic way, would counter that he might not be alive today if he had embraced that style of racing.

Unlike some Formula 1 drivers, who were more or less born into a car seat, Prost was 14 before he got his first taste of competitive driving, when his father introduced him to karting during a family holiday. He was a quick learner and was a full-time racer by 1974 and a karting champion by 1975. He won championships at Formula Renault France and Formula Renault Europe before taking the French and European Formula 3 titles in 1979.

At the time, McLaren were in the doldrums after two world championships in the 1970s. Emerson Fittipaldi had won the title in 1974, with James Hunt following in 1976. With McLaren's fortunes on the ebb, Prost's victory in the 1979 Monaco F3 race earned him a test drive with the team.

It went well – although possibly a mere fable, legend has it that team principal Teddy Mayer jogged to his car to retrieve a draft contract for the Frenchman. If true, Mayer must have liked what he saw very much as he was not known for his fondness for exercise.

INTO FORMULA 1

It was an easy nickname to give a driver of slight build. Prost would become known as 'Le Professeur' later in his career, but during his first year in Formula 1, driving for a McLaren team on the verge of a radical transformation, he was 'Little Napper'. McLaren manager Tony Jardine is credited with coming up with the name, but Prost never felt quite as French as Napoleon, and would later wonder if the fact he achieved all his greatest successes with English teams was something to do with that.

Prost was an easy-going personality, which helped him ride out the ribbing from Jardine that might have rubbed another driver up the wrong way. Not only did he call Prost Little Napper, he would also shout 'get the oxygen out!' when Prost arrived in the morning, suggesting that everyone else would be fighting for air now Prost's large nose had arrived on the scene.

Although Prost would have to deal with prickly and even hostile teammates later in his career, he was fortunate in his first season. John Watson was a calm presence, much like a good-natured big brother, who did not feel threatened or jealous despite Prost's obvious talent.

Prost won his first point in his first race, finishing sixth in Argentina, and followed up with fifth place in Brazil. It was a golden era for French drivers, with four Frenchmen winning a total of five Grand Prix between them in 1980, but Prost was not among those winners. He ended the season with just five points, following two more sixth-place finishes. Encouragingly, he was just a point behind the vastly more experienced Watson.

Changes were already afoot at McLaren, with Ron Dennis and John Barnard eager to revolutionise the team. Barnard would introduce the MP4, with the first carbon-fibre composite chassis seen in the sport, but Prost would not be driving it in 1981. He was headed for Renault.

THE RENAULT YEARS

It seemed a natural fit – an up-and-coming French driver at a French team – and Prost also had a French teammate in

René Arnoux, but the marriage was not a happy one. The 1981 season got off to a disastrous start, with Prost failing to finish in six of the first seven races, but his fortunes changed at his home Grand Prix. Victory at Dijon was Prost's first in Formula 1, and he followed with two more to finish the year in fifth place in the Drivers' Championship, just seven points behind champion Nelson Piquet.

Prost had shown he belonged, but the next season would teach him valuable lessons and transform the way he drove for the rest of his career. Gilles Villeneuve and Didier Pironi became embroiled in a dispute over team orders, with Villeneuve losing his cool entirely. "He was absolutely out of control," Prost commented on the Canadian's mood at the 1982 Belgian Grand Prix.

Apparently determined to better Pironi's time in qualifying, Villeneuve suffered fatal injuries in a crash. The season also claimed the life of young Italian racer Riccardo Paletti, and Pironi was involved in a career-ending accident in heavy rain. Prost, one of the first to reach Pironi as he lay in the mangled wreckage of his car, was deeply affected.

"Everybody thinks that I don't like driving in the wet," Prost commented, "but it was almost my preference before this. I realised this day that I had to be more careful."

From that moment, Prost refused to push himself to his

⌄ Back with the McLaren team, with new teammate Lauda, in 1984

limit. It undoubtedly cost him time and may well have cost him wins, but it also allowed him to walk away from the sport in one piece. Prost's new philosophy on driving was in direct contrast to that of a driver like Senna, with whom the Frenchman would soon embark on a fierce and sometimes bitter rivalry. It is also fundamental to the man's 'official' nickname, Le Professeur. As commentating legend Murray Walker said: "Alain was a master tactician. He thought it all out and drove as fast as he needed to drive."

Prost himself put it a little differently, in a statement that is unusually candid for a Formula 1 driver. "I'm very realistic," he said. "I know when I'm competitive and I know when I'm not."

Of course, Prost was competitive far more often than not. In 1983, he was in control of the Drivers' Championship, winning four races and looking comfortable before his car let him down. Failure to finish in three of the last four races, coupled with a strong finish by Piquet, gave the title to the Brazilian by just two points. A turbo failure knocked Prost out of the last race, when the title was still within his grasp, and he had to settle for second place. Clearly, he was a man on the rise, but Renault needed a scapegoat for failing to win a title – and that scapegoat was Prost. He was let go from the team, but it turned out to be the best thing that could have happened.

RETURN TO MCLAREN

McLaren were entering a period of dominance. New rules for 1984 prevented refuelling during a race, and the team had an efficient Porsche engine. Coupled with Prost's considered

'Le Professeur' embraced a conservative style of racing that won him four world championships

approach to driving, it was a devastating combination that carried the Frenchman to seven Grand Prix victories.

But Prost was not alone at McLaren. He had come in as officially the number two driver to Niki Lauda and the Austrian, though not as steady as Prost, was a still formidable force. He won five races to push Prost all the way, but although the championship was still up for grabs on the last day of the season, its outcome had actually been decided way back in the sixth race.

Heavy rain had turned the streets of Monaco into an extended swimming pool, and Prost had gestured from his cockpit that the race ought to be stopped for safety reasons. At that point he was leading but Senna, revelling in the wet, was eating up his lead at a frightening rate. The race was eventually stopped, and although Prost was awarded the win, he was only given half the usual points because the drivers had not completed at least 75 per cent of the race. Those lost four-and-a-half points would go on to prove crucial on the last weekend of the season, at Portugal.

Prost and Lauda had dominated the closing stages of the season. For the previous six races they had alternated wins

– Lauda, Prost, Lauda, Prost, Lauda, Prost – but although Prost broke the cycle by claiming his seventh win of the season, Lauda finished second, just enough to snatch the title by half a point. It was the second straight season that Prost had lost the championship on the last race, and a rumour circulated that McLaren had printed posters to acclaim his first world title.

There would be no last-gasp drama in 1985. Prost cruised to his first championship, benefitting from a late-season collapse by Italian Michele Alboreto (the Ferrari driver failed to finish the last four races) to win by 20 points. As the season wound down to its rather anticlimactic conclusion, Prost took the opportunity to fly to the Vatican for a personal audience with Pope John Paul II. Although it is easy to caricature Prost as a man of science, especially in contrast to the deeply spiritual Senna, Prost was in fact a man with his own strong faith. He just did not allow it to intrude upon his racing style.

Prost had officially secured the title at Brands Hatch, in the European Grand Prix. Needing to finish at least fifth to be uncatchable, he crossed the line in fourth, although it is unclear what he thought about the wasted effort of finishing one place higher than necessary.

Prost was awarded the Légion d'honneur for becoming the first Frenchman to win the Formula 1 Drivers' Championship, but despite this, he never felt like he was a national hero. He

Prost in the Williams battles with Senna in the McLaren in 1993

did not court fame, and when it came calling nonetheless during his near-miss 1983 season, his response was to promptly move to Switzerland to get away from it. Even now, as a world champion, he did not feel completely accepted, saying, "Sometimes I never felt one hundred per cent French, to be honest."

Fortune appeared to be on Prost's side in 1986, although he had to cope with the tragedy of losing his brother to cancer during the season. Four racers were in contention as the season wound down, with Prost, Nigel Mansell, Piquet and Senna all in the hunt. Mansell appeared to have the championship sewn up until he suffered a blowout at nearly 200mph (322km/h) in the final race at Adelaide. That put his Williams teammate, Piquet, in position to win the championship, but Williams could not risk him also suffering a blowout and he was called in to change tyres.

Prost found himself in the lead but was worryingly low on fuel. His onboard computer said he would not make the finish line, but he defied it in order to win his second straight title, although he pulled to a halt immediately after taking the chequered flag – whether through choice or because he had run out of fuel is not known.

THE SENNA RIVALRY

In 1987, Prost was pushed down to fourth place as Williams made their move towards prominence, and McLaren were looking for a new teammate for the two-time champion going into 1988. The season did hold one highlight, as Prost

won his third Grand Prix of the season at Portugal, taking his career total to 28 and setting a new record.

Prost was in favour of Senna joining McLaren for 1988, preferring an up-and-coming driver to the other hot candidate, reigning world champion Piquet. Prost got his way, but it became the embodiment of the phrase 'be careful what you wish for'. Senna immediately ruffled feathers and won the 1988 title, with Prost striking back in 1989 to secure his third championship.

Much is made of the fact that Prost was a superior politician to Senna, but it was the Frenchman who found himself manoeuvred out at McLaren. "I was driven out by Senna," Prost would later claim, "by Honda a little bit… and by Ron [Dennis]." The relationship between the two men, if anything, worsened after Prost left for Ferrari. After they collided at the first corner at the Japanese Grand Prix, knocking them both out of the race, Prost commented: "I wanted to punch him in the face, but I was so disgusted I could not do it. He revolts me."

It was a difficult time for Prost. Unhappy with the team setup at Ferrari, he fell to fifth in the Drivers' Championship in 1991 as Senna won his third and final title. Making matters worse, Prost was outspoken in his criticism of Ferrari and found himself sacked before the final race of the year. "Ferrari does not deserve to be world champion," he had said. "It is a team without directive and without strategy." Prost also fell out with the Italian media, who were highly influential, and the last straw seems to have been when he described the beloved Ferrari racing car as a "truck". To be fair, Prost was referring to the way the car handled after its shock absorbers had failed, but out of context the insult was too much for Ferrari to stand.

 Senna leads Prost at Imola in 1989

"Maybe the mistake I made was believing I could change the mentality, the way they work and approach problems," Prost said. Whatever the mistake had been, he was once more looking for a new team.

THE LAST HURRAH

Prost was forced to sit out 1992, which saw the Williams-Renault team put together a season of remarkable dominance. With the team's highly advanced car taking much of the plaudits, Mansell won his first and only world title, beating teammate Riccardo Patrese into second place by a gaudy 52 points. The following season, Prost was back, behind the wheel of the all-conquering Williams car. Seven wins in the first ten races allowed him to cruise to his fourth and final championship, beating Senna by 26 points.

Knowing Senna was likely to join Williams the following season, and lacking the appetite to find yet another new team, Prost retired after his fourth title. He also felt personally hurt that so much credit for his final championship was being given to the Williams car.

Not quite finished with the sport, Prost dabbled in running his own team, Prost Grand Prix, but later admitted to getting cold feet almost straight away. Nevertheless, he pushed on long enough to rack up huge losses before deciding to bow out in 2002.

Prost had proven that a racing driver did not need to have the mindset of a First World War fighter pilot. His considered, pragmatic approach to racing, coupled with the fact that he never looked as fast as he actually was, made him less eye-catching than the barnstormers of Formula 1, but the results were unequivocal – his record of 51 Grand Prix victories would stand until 2001, when Michael Schumacher would surpass it. McLaren team coordinator Jo Ramirez perhaps summed up Prost's style best when commenting on his inspection of the two McLaren cars following the 1986 Australian Grand Prix, where Prost had won his second title: "I remember looking afterwards at the brakes on both of our cars," Ramirez said. "There was no way Keke [Rosberg] could have done another ten laps... Alain could probably have done another race... he was so gentle on the brakes, on the tyres, the gears, everything."

It was a distinctive way of driving, from a distinctive man who liked to stay within his own limits and those of his car, trusting nothing to fate. It is unsurprising, therefore, that his autobiography is titled, Maître de Mon Destin ('Master of My Own Destiny').

KIMI RÄIKKÖNEN
THE ICE MAN

The unfazeable 'Iceman' who triumphed in one of the closest finales in F1 history

Kimi Räikkönen found himself on the fast track to F1, landing a seat at Sauber having only competed in 23 Formula Ford and Formula Renault races. Despite the misgivings of the authorities, the 21 year old was granted a licence to race and steered his car home in sixth place to score his first point. It later emerged that Räikkönen had been napping 30 minutes before the race began. The Iceman – cool and monosyllabic off the track, unflappable and reliable on it – had arrived.

McLaren saw Räikkönen as the heir to fellow Finn Mika Häkkinen. After helping Sauber to fourth place in the Constructors' Championship, Räikkönen was snapped up by Ron Dennis and teamed up with David Coulthard. Although the move to McLaren gave Räikkönen a faster ride, his new team were plagued by unreliability and inconsistency. Nevertheless, the next five years saw Räikkönen pick up nine wins, 36 podiums and two second-place finishes in the Drivers' Championship, in 2003 and 2005.

Räikkönen replaced another retiring champion in 2007, joining Ferrari to take over Michael Schumacher's seat. He started well, winning the first Grand Prix from pole position, and ended just as impressively, winning the final two races. That final victory allowed Räikkönen to leapfrog McLaren's Lewis Hamilton and Fernando Alonso in the standings, giving him the Drivers' Championship by a single point.

Räikkönen never mounted another challenge for the title, although he did earn three third-place finishes and drove well for Ferrari, Lotus and Alfa Romeo. He dismissed team instructions en route to his only win with Lotus with a curt "Leave me alone. I know what I'm doing". He wasn't wrong – few drivers could call on the experience the Iceman could. He retired in 2021 with the record for the most Grand Prix.

» Räikkönen driving the McLaren MP4-19B at Silverstone, 2 June 2004

INFO

Nationality
Finnish

Teams
Sauber (2001)
McLaren (2002–2006)
Ferrari (2007–2009,
2014–2018)
Lotus (2012–2013)
Alfa Romeo (2019–2021)

Championships
1 (2007)

Number of races
349

Number of race wins
21

Number of podiums
103

Pole positions
18

INFO

Nationality
German

Teams
Williams (2006–2009)
Mercedes (2010–2016)

Championships
1 (2016)

Number of races
206

Number of race wins
23

Number of podiums
57

Pole positions
30

NICO ROSBERG
ONE AND OUT

How Mercedes driver Nico Rosberg gave F1 fans the ultimate mic drop moment by achieving a life-long dream and then quitting the sport

Few of us mere mortals are destined for greatness. Even fewer achieve that greatness. Nico Rosberg is one of those privileged few that had huge expectations placed on him from birth and managed to meet those expectations in style.

Rosberg was born in Wiesbaden, Germany in 1985, son of German Sina Rosberg and Finnish 1982 Formula 1 World Drivers' Champion Keke Rosberg. So there was quite some pressure on his shoulders right from the start.

Rosberg's parents gently encouraged him as he took his first tentative steps into motor racing. He took the well-trodden path of earning his stripes in karting, starting at the tender age of six. By the turn of the century he had progressed to Formula A Karting Championships, where he would become the teammate of a certain, highly competitive lad from Stevenage by the name of Lewis Hamilton, but more on him later. Rosberg was quiet but ultra competitive and this steely determination helped him rise through the junior ranks. He won the 2002 Formula BMW ADAC Series, which earned him a test drive at Williams, the team with which his father had won the world championship 20 years previously. The stars were beginning to align for Rosberg's pursuit of his destiny.

He continued to progress and impress, claiming the first-ever GP2 title in 2005. Interestingly the man who succeeded him as GP2 champion was Hamilton, but, again, more on him later.

The following year, Rosberg got his chance. A spot opened up at Williams alongside experienced Australian Mark Webber and Rosberg was literally in the driving seat. The rookie had a successful first race for the Williams team, claiming the fastest lap, finishing seventh and earning two points. He was plagued with reliability issues, recording seven DNFs, but only finished three points behind Webber.

The 2007 season was an improvement for Rosberg, outscoring new teammate Alexander Wurz by 20 points to 13. No doubt he was looking on enviously at the McLaren team where debutant Hamilton finished joint second in the championship behind Kimi Räikkönen.

In 2010 Rosberg got the move that would change his life. Brawn Mercedes, who the year before had romped to the Constructors' Championship with Jenson Button and Rubens Barrichello, had rebranded as Mercedes and were clearly looking for a German pairing. Even though Rosberg was born to a Finnish father and lived in Monaco, he had chosen to represent the country of his mother and his birth, so was the perfect driver for the new team. Not only that, but Mercedes had managed to lure seven-time champion Michael Schumacher out of retirement for one last hurrah. Rosberg had secured a drive at the reigning Constructors'

« Rosberg celebrates with his team after becoming the 2016 F1 World Drivers Champion

⌃ The 1982 Formula 1 world champion, Keke Rosberg, posing with Nico, the 2016 Formula 1 world champion

Champions alongside the greatest champion of all time. Things were certainly looking up. Rosberg had a strong season, finishing seventh in the driver standings, with nearly double the points tally of his illustrious teammate. Progress continued into 2012 where victory in China earned him a maiden Grand Prix win. However, he would go on to claim one more podium place that season as he finished the season ninth.

Then, ahead of the 2013 season, a dramatic moment. Schumacher retired for good, leaving a seat alongside Rosberg at Mercedes. Into that seat slipped Hamilton, who had shocked the Formula 1 world by leaving a McLaren team he had been at his entire professional life. In doing so he reunited with Rosberg a decade after they had previously shared a garage. Rosberg won two races to Hamilton's one, but both were blown away by Sebastian Vettel in the Red Bull. That one-sided championship ushered in a new age of Formula 1 – the hybrid era. New power units used a hybrid energy recovery system aimed at making the sport greener and more sustainable. This played right into the hands of Mercedes who simply destroyed the competition. Rosberg and Hamilton won 16 of the 19 races, meaning it was simply a matter of which driver would take individual glory. After an intense fight, the championship was in the balance going into the final race in Abu Dhabi, which controversially had double points on offer. Despite starting on pole, the German got off to the worst possible start as Hamilton burned past him off the start line. Things went from bad to worse when Rosberg started losing power midway through the race and he limped home in 14th. Second place in the championship

marked a huge upturn in fortunes, but he was still short of that coveted title.

The pattern was similar the following season, but by this point tensions were running very high in the Mercedes paddock. Hamilton again had the advantage over Rosberg, winning ten races, the last of which was the US Grand Prix. Rosberg had been leading the race until a late error gave Hamilton the win he needed to take the title. This emotionally damaging defeat proved to be the catalyst for Rosberg to set about changing his fortunes, as he promptly hired a sports psychologist to help him work through the mental block that was preventing him from getting one over his rival. This fix clearly worked as Rosberg won the final three races of the season to secure a consecutive runners-up place in the championship.

However, second places weren't enough to feed Rosberg's burning, insatiable desire to win the championship. He had to balance this with an emerging family life, having married girlfriend Vivian in 2014, who had given birth to their daughter Alaïa in 2015. Despite, or maybe because of this, Rosberg threw himself totally into his work for the 2016 season, dropping everything from leg muscle to sock size in order to minimise his in-car weight. He worked for two hours a day with his sports psychologist in a bid to marry mental toughness with physical perfection. This attitude paid dividends as he won the first four races of the season before a collision with Hamilton on the first lap of the Spanish Grand Prix knocked both out and ended his streak. Hamilton hit back, winning six of the next seven races, but Rosberg's new-found mental strength meant he was undeterred, winning four of the next five to move clear in the title race. Hamilton won the next three, meaning that Rosberg was just 12 points clear heading into the final race in Abu Dhabi. Hamilton was on pole and controlled the race, with Rosberg holding onto the

▼ Rosberg's first drive in Formula 1 came with his father's team, Williams

second place that would win him the title. In a desperate bid to take the championship, Hamilton slowed his pace, pushing Rosberg back into traffic in the hope he would be overtaken and Hamilton would retain the title. However, a masterful display of driving kept Rosberg in second and when he crossed the line, he had achieved that lifelong ambition of becoming the world champion, 34 years after his father. Five days later he shocked the world by announcing he would be retiring from the sport. He revealed in interviews the toll that the season had taken on him as he gave everything he could in pursuit of his dream. He said: "Through the hard work, the pain, the sacrifices, this has been my target. And now I've made it. I have climbed the mountain, I have reached the peak. This feels right." The family for whom he had sacrificed so much and who had sacrificed so much for him were able to welcome back a husband, a father and a world champion. And for a man who wanted so much to emulate his own father, maybe that was an even sweeter reward. Rosberg had his one title and was out, but the way he achieved that dream makes him a legend of the sport.

« Rosberg celebrates winning the 2016 Drivers' Championship in style after the Abu Dhabi Grand Prix

THE BATTLE ROYALE

Not since the days of Alain Prost and Ayrton Senna have two teammates battled each other so fiercely for the Formula 1 title. Rosberg and Hamilton's first season as a pair passed with little drama, but the following year, when both were streets ahead of the competition, the rivalry really took hold. In Bahrain, the third race of the season, the duo went wheel-to-wheel in a thrilling duel, won by Hamilton. In Monaco, Hamilton complained that Rosberg deliberately ran his car off the road to prevent Hamilton setting a faster qualifying lap, but then in Hungary Hamilton got revenge, refusing to let Rosberg pass, potentially costing the German victory. Tensions really came to a head in Belgium where Rosberg lost the lead to Hamilton, then clipped him going into a corner, forcing Hamilton to retire. Rosberg was booed on the podium and was forced to apologise to his teammate. Things were no better in 2015 with the infamous Capgate incident, where Hamilton, having benefitted from a Rosberg error to clinch a championship-winning victory in the USA, chucked the runners-up hat at Rosberg who tetchily flung it back at Hamilton with interest. Into 2016 and collisions in Spain and Austria caused both drivers to lose championship points, earning them both a dressing down from team principal Toto Wolff.

Despite the dramas, Rosberg led going into the final race of 2016 and, in clear defiance of team orders, Hamilton did everything he possibly could to back his teammate into the chasing pack, hoping that would lose Rosberg places, points and the championship. He failed, Rosberg won the title, retired and the world was denied the drama of a fourth chapter in the saga between the drivers.

INFO

Nationality
German

Teams
Jordan (1991)
Benetton (1991–1995)
Ferrari (1996–2006)
Mercedes (2010–2012)

Championships
7 (1994, 1995, 2000, 2001, 2002, 2003, 2004)

Number of races
306

Number of race wins
91

Number of podiums
155

Pole positions
68

MICHAEL SCHUMACHER

THE RED BARON

Ruthless, dedicated, determined – Michael Schumacher was all of these, which is perhaps why he is one of the best drivers ever in Formula 1

s Michael Schumacher the GOAT (Greatest Of All Time)? Lots of people certainly claim he is, and those who do argue that the sheer weight of his achievements overwhelms any thoughts that possibly Ayrton Senna or Alain Prost were more artistic, or that Juan Manuel Fangio was the best, albeit in an entirely different era. But if statistics are the only measure, then Lewis Hamilton has equalled or broken most of Schumacher's records.

Hamilton now has the same number of world titles and has more race wins, more podium finishes and more points (even when adjusted to the current era). So where does that leave Schumacher in the all-time rankings? Still pretty close to the top, although the GOAT title is always going to be a subjective one. It's not just because of his seven world championships – won for two different teams – but his five-in-a-row for Ferrari is still a record that even Hamilton is unlikely to beat. For a period, Schumacher was nigh-on unbeatable when it really mattered.

It all began in the same manner in which many drivers take their first steps – karting. For Schumacher, though, it was often a case of make do and mend; he never had the money to afford the best karting equipment so he had to buy and borrow what he could. Although his father, Rolf, ran the kart track where the family lived, he was a bricklayer by trade and money was never plentiful. He claims he never had any long-time plan about progressing through the various forms of racing, or that he ever really thought about Formula 1. He just went karting because he enjoyed it, and found he was good enough at it that people were prepared to pay him to do it. In fact, so much did Schumacher enjoy karts, that even as F1 world champion he would sometimes spend time in the off-season racing them, or testing the tyres on them, for free. Part of it is that Schumacher is obsessive over details, whatever vehicle he happens to be in. Reams have been written about the German ace's involvement in the smallest details, such as how, when at Benetton, he had a speedometer in his car so he could check for himself which was the quickest racing line to take. And once he got to Formula 1 he loved all the driver aids, such as traction control, and would spend many hours tinkering and fine-tuning until he was satisfied that he had maximised their advantages.

Ross Brawn once indicated that Schumacher was so good he could manoeuvre round any problem. "We actually learnt more from [the likes of] Eddie Irvine or Rubens Barrichello," he

» Schumacher celebrating with teammates after winning the 2004 F1 Drivers' Championship

said. "With them, we could always tell if there was a problem by looking at lap times." Schumacher, on the other hand, would be fast and consistent even when there was an issue – he would just work out ways around it.

A RACING LIFE

But first, let's backtrack a little. Schumacher won the German kart title before he even held an official karting licence (too young to apply for a German licence, he got one in Luxembourg instead). By 1987, he was the European kart champion as well, and the following year, he made his first debut in single-seat car racing by participating in the German Formula Ford series.

In 1989, Schumacher signed with Willi Weber's WTS Formula Three team and competed in the German Formula Three series. Thus began a lifelong association with Weber, who owned a management company and became Schumacher's manager. Schumacher won the Formula Three title in 1990 and the same year he joined the Mercedes junior racing programme in the World Sportscar Championship. This was an unusual step, recommended by Weber, who thought that long-distance races in powerful cars would benefit Schumacher's career. He only ever competed in one Formula 3000 race, considered the more obvious route to F1 for aspiring drivers. That was in the Japanese Formula 3000 Championship in 1991; he finished second. He also drove in Le Mans that year as it was part

of the World Sportscar Championship, finishing fifth with teammates Karl Wendlinger and Fritz Kreutzpointner.

Schumacher's F1 debut came about in the strangest of ways, at the 1991 Belgian Grand Prix. Jordan driver Bertrand Gachot was convicted of actual bodily harm following an altercation with a taxi driver who he sprayed with CS gas. Although Gachot's initial 18-month sentence was later reduced to two months, it left team boss Eddie Jordan searching for a replacement driver at short notice. Schumacher got the nod, and immediately impressed. It is occasionally forgotten that his race actually only lasted until the second corner, when mechanical failure in the Jordan ended it. However, it was in qualifying that Schumacher caught the eye. He qualified in seventh, which was a season's best for a Jordan and higher than the experienced Andrea de Cesaris managed.

Jordan saw Schumacher was a star in the making, and tried to sign him. Unfortunately for the maverick Irishman he was far from the only team boss to realise that, and the flamboyant Flavio Briatore snatched him away for Benetton at the 11th hour.

F1 STARDOM

Schumacher's move into Formula 1 was complete at the start of the 1992 season, but for the next two years it was Williams who dominated, not Benetton. Not only did they have a supremely fast car powered by excellent Renault engines, they also had one fully equipped with semi-automatic gearboxes and active suspension. It wasn't until 1993 that Benetton introduced their own active suspension and traction control, the last of the major teams to do so. In 1994, it looked like Benetton had cracked it, with Schumacher winning six of the first seven races (and finishing second in the other). But then disaster struck. Benetton were investigated for breaking the governing body's new rules on electronic aids. They were eventually exonerated, but only on the technical grounds that there was no evidence that the form of launch control software found, which was illegal, had actually been employed.

Next, came the first signs of Schumacher's desire to win at all costs. First he was disqualified from the British Grand Prix for ignoring a black flag, and banned for two races. Then,

Schumacher racing karts at Kerpen, Germany, in 1994

on his return, he was disqualified from the Belgian Grand Prix, after winning it, for illegal wear on the skidblock. (The skidblock is a 10mm thick wooden plank which prevents the cars from running low enough to contact the track surface; this skid block is measured before and after a race and if it's found to be less than 9mm thick after the race, the car is disqualified.)

Schumacher missed the next two races, in Italy and Portugal, which enabled Damon Hill to close the gap at the top of the standings to just a single point going into the final race in Australia.

Schumacher was always in front of Hill in Adelaide, but the Briton kept sufficiently close to maintain the pressure and on

lap 36, the German ran too wide on a left-hand corner and hit the wall. His race was over, Hill would be the champion. Except as Hill came round the same bend a couple of seconds later, Schumacher hit him and Hill's Williams was also too badly damaged to continue. Was it deliberate? It's impossible to say for certain, however many times one watches the replay. Hill was certainly magnanimous in defeat, saying he needed to get two points to become world champion, and didn't. End of story. Others were less sanguine, with British fans and the British media opining that it was a calculated move. Hill was hugely popular in the UK, and this incident might have been coloured by the general perceptions of the two men.

It was a different story in 1995. Schumacher was in control more or less throughout the year, winning his second world title and also helping Benetton to the Constructors' Championship for the first time. It was clear Benetton couldn't hold onto their prize asset; Schumacher looked around and, in typically clinical fashion, decided that Ferrari offered him the best opportunity.

THE FERRARI YEARS

A year after he had signed for Ferrari, Schumacher managed to lure Ross Brawn and Rory Byrne into following him, reuniting the 'dream team' from Benetton. Jean Todt had been team boss since July 1993, and together these four men set about making Ferrari great again. Todt's genius lay in uniting a previously fractured team, though the car itself remained stubbornly uncompetitive for Schumacher's first couple of seasons.

Schumacher was fast, undoubtedly, but the Ferrari was not yet reliable enough over the course of a long season. Schumacher won races and in 1999 he helped Ferrari to their first Constructors' Championship since 1983, but a broken leg suffered at the high-speed Stowe Corner at Silverstone ruled him out for three months and cost him a realistic shot at the Drivers' crown.

It wasn't until 2000 that the entire package came together

Schumacher leading the pack on the opening lap of the 2006 Chinese Grand Prix

and swept Schumacher to his third title, and his first with Ferrari. Four more were to follow over successive seasons, with Ferrari also taking the Constructors' title on each occasion. Schumacher said later that the 2000 title was the one that mattered: "[It] is the one that means the most to me. Everything that came after was a bonus." Schumacher could never exactly be described as carefree, but certainly it appeared that a weight had been lifted. The next three seasons saw Ferrari in charge, and Schumacher recorded 39 of his 91 Grand Prix victories over the period from 2001 to 2004. But it was the 2004 season when we witnessed driver and car in perfect harmony. Schumacher won 12 of the first 13 races in the championship that year, missing out only in Monaco where he clashed with Juan Pablo Montoya. He added another triumph in Japan, meaning he had won 13 out of 18 races; since teammate Rubens Barrichello won in

It took the dream team of Jean Todt, Ross Brawn and Schumacher a few years to work out Ferrari's problems – and solve them in spectacular fashion

THE SON ALSO RISES

The awful fate that befell Michael Schumacher on 29 December 2013 in Méribel in the French Alps has had a profound effect on the sporting world. In more recent years we have seen fatal accidents in F1 all but eliminated, so it seems deeply ironic that one of the greatest of all time suffered his worst injury away from the track. His son Mick, 14 at the time, was with his father that day and was already a racing driver. Keen not to be seen to be cashing in on the family name, or the privileges it might bestow, Mick Schumacher began his career using his mother Corinna's maiden name of Betsch. Like his father, he had started in karts before moving successfully through Formula 4, Formula 3 (winning the European title in 2018) and Formula 2, which he won in 2020.

Mick made his Formula 1 debut for Haas in the first race of the 2021 season, the Bahrain Grand Prix, and continued with the team through 2022. Haas was, sadly, not competitive but he managed to secure 12 points from 43 races, with his best result a sixth-place finish at the 2022 Austrian Grand Prix. In 2023, Mick signed for Mercedes as reserve driver. Perhaps more significantly, he also served as reserve driver for Ferrari from 2019 to 2022 – expect to see him driving for the Prancing Horse his father did so much to revitalise before too many seasons are out. It would be a very welcome codicil to the Schumacher story.

Mick Schumacher making his debut at Ferrari, as designated test driver during the 2019 in-season testing

 Ferrari crushed all the opposition in 2004

Italy and China. There were only three races in the entire season that were not won by a Ferrari. This is an almost unbelievable level of consistency, particularly for a car that only a few years earlier was the epitome of unreliability.

RETURNING TO THE MOTHER LAND

Intriguingly, there was a time when Schumacher thought his Ferrari years were only one part of his career. As a former Mercedes junior, and a German to boot, the lure of the marque was significant and a serious approach was made in 1998. But ultimately, Schumacher and Todt made a good team – they were similarly work-obsessed and had the same views on how an F1 team functioned. On the other hand, Ron Dennis at Mercedes had a slightly different style, about which Schumacher said: "There might have been a way to work with Mercedes, but not with Ron Dennis. Our points of view on how a team works were just too different." It was not until Schumacher came out of his first retirement (which lasted four seasons) that he eventually made the journey back to Mercedes.

By then it was a new team, with Ross Brawn as team principal. Many felt Schumacher might be past it, though Damon Hill warned, "you should never write Schumacher off." As it turns out, he was not able to add to his tally of race victories in his three seasons with Mercedes; the car was not comparable with the Red Bull that dominated the Constructors' Championship in those years. It was

frustrating for such a born winner as Schumacher to be held back by inadequate cars, and by the end of the 2012 season he retired for good. Hamilton replaced him, going on to equal or break many of Schumacher's records over the next seven years, in the Mercedes.

THE SCHUMACHER STYLE

There are so many examples of Schumacher's phenomenal skill that it's impossible to pick them all out. His 1995 victory at Spa when he started in 16th. His first win for Ferrari in 1996, when he mastered the pouring rain and showed for the first time what a threat he was going to be in bad weather conditions. The 1998 Hungarian Grand Prix where he made up 25 seconds in 19 laps to take victory. The Malaysian Grand Prix in 2001, which he won despite a catastrophic 72-second pit stop. And then there were the duels with other fine drivers: Damon Hill, Gilles Villeneuve, Mika Häkkinen, Fernando Alonso – all of them world championship-winning drivers themselves.

How much did these victories owe to Schumacher's single-mindedness? The psychology of Michael Schumacher is an interesting study. As has been mentioned, he liked to be closely involved with all aspects of preparing and testing a car, and he often talked about being one part of a highly skilled team that was chasing the same dream. His perfectionist tendencies were all too clear, and

» Schumacher steers his car during the 2012 Brazilian Grand Prix at Interlagos. It would be his last race in Formula 1

he has spoken of how he approached every corner with the intention of taking it on as fast as was humanly possible. Rival drivers have pointed to his ability to compartmentalise and focus utterly on the task at hand.

Hill, who competed against Schumacher more than most, once said that Schumacher seemed able to shut off his emotional side while in a car and bend it to his iron will. "If sport is to have any worth, then there are certain human values which have to be observed. It is only then that a victory or a championship can be rated as a great achievement," said Hill. "I think that idea baffles Michael."

Take a look at Schumacher as he strides towards his car on race day, locked and loaded. Totally focused. Taking a car to its limit is just what he does, it comes so naturally to him that – like a lot of world-class sportspeople – he can't actually put it into words. He can't explain what he is feeling, because he isn't actually feeling anything except a oneness with the car. Schumacher himself has offered the opinion that what he could promise was "consistency. Lap times weren't good one day then bad the next. I believe the information I provide needs to be clear and rational, not clouded with emotion."

A LASTING IMPACT

Looking back at Schumacher's career, it's interesting to examine what impact he had on Formula 1. His legacy to Ferrari is that he made them great again. It is as simple as that. For the world's greatest car marque, and the most successful F1 team of all-time, it was vital that they got back to winning ways after a painful period in the wilderness.

On a more personal level, Schumacher undoubtedly sparked German interest in F1. Previously something of a niche sport in his home country, it became hugely popular and even though he moved his family to Switzerland to avoid the punitive tax regime in Germany, Schumacher always enjoyed the support of his fellow Germans. When he retired for the first time, in 2006, three of the top ten drivers in that year's standings were German. Sebastian Vettel, himself a four-time world champion, has said that Schumacher was a key inspiration for his own F1 career.

The tragic skiing accident that almost killed Schumacher in 2013 is not a conclusion befitting one of the greatest of sportspeople. Fans of F1, of motorsport and indeed sport of any kind will know that this colossus of racing deserves so much more than that.

INFO

Nationality
Brazilian

Teams
Toleman (1984)
Lotus (1985–1987)
McLaren (1988–1993)
Williams (1994)

Championships
3 (1988, 1990, 1991)

Number of races
161

Number of race wins
41

Number of podiums
80

Pole positions
65

AYRTON SENNA
MAN OF GOD

Revered by many as the greatest driver of all time, Ayrton Senna set new standards in the sport

Ayrton Senna da Silva appears to have been destined to race for a living. At the age of four he was driving karts. At nine he was behind the wheel of a Jeep. At 13, he was racing. He always knew what the primary purpose of his life was, but this did not mean he ignored all other responsibilities. He was level-headed enough to realise he needed to work hard at school so that he could devote his time to his driving when he got home.

Competing in karting, in a sport without the contaminating influences of money or politics, he enjoyed a purity of racing that he was not to find again, but his trajectory was inevitably upwards. In 1981 he won the English Formula Ford 1600 Championship and two years later the British Formula 3 title. By this time he had adopted his mother's maiden name, Senna, as da Silva was so common it did not give him the distinctiveness he desired.

Despite his parents' wishes that he join the family business, Senna was clearly headed in a different direction.

FORMULA 1

Toleman-Hart were not a glamorous name in the world of Formula 1, but with other teams not quite interested enough to offer him a seat, they would have to do. A small team with limited aspirations, they posed no threat of winning podium places or troubling the big teams of the day. Senna's debut race, fittingly enough in Brazil, lasted just eight laps, but in his second outing, in South Africa, he finished sixth to win his first Drivers' Championship point.

This first completed race was a sobering experience. Accustomed to much shorter races in Formula 3 and Formula Ford, the two hours he spent in the cockpit in the

heat at Kyalami, in the Transvaal, were physically and mentally exhausting. Senna had announced himself to the F1 world, but he proved he belonged in his sixth race, in vastly different conditions.

The Monte Carlo Grand Prix saw him line up alongside such names as Alain Prost, Keke Rosberg, Niki Lauda and Nigel Mansell, all past or future world champions. Senna started in 13th place, but demonstrated what was to be one of his trademarks – mastery of wet driving conditions – as he moved up through the field. He passed Lauda to move into second place and was catching the leader, Prost, at a phenomenal rate when the race was stopped on the 31st lap, just as he was poised to take the lead. Nevertheless, a podium finish was a dramatic statement of intent.

The decision to stop the race, handing victory to Prost, was the first time the two men came into conflict in their careers. It would not be the last.

» Senna's extraordinary race in appalling conditions at Monaco in 1984

THE MOVE TO LOTUS

Toleman had given Senna his chance in F1, but it was clear he needed a bigger team. Lotus made sense and he was highly competitive in 1985, winning four pole positions in the first six races. However, he could only convert those into one win, following another triumphant drive in the rain in Portugal. Over the full season he earned three more poles, but was forced to retire seven times and finished fourth in the Drivers' Championship with 38 points as Prost took his first world title comfortably.

In the next season, although Prost remained the front-runner and target for the rest of the field, it was the Brazilian head-to-head of Senna and Nelson Piquet that was the most intriguing storyline. It was a similar story to 1985, as Senna earned eight pole positions (including the first three of the season) but only managed two wins. He finished fourth again, 14 points behind his countryman, while Prost won his second consecutive title.

Senna's third and final season with Lotus saw him improve to third in the final standings in a season dominated by the one-two punch of the Williams team, courtesy of Piquet and Mansell. Piquet ultimately won the title and it was clear Senna needed to move again if he was to take the next step in his career.

THE GLORY YEARS

If 1987 had been a Mansell-Piquet story, 1988 was even more focused on two drivers. Now teammates at McLaren, Senna and Prost won 15 out of the 16 races to finish in the top two spots of the Drivers' Championship. Prost displayed all his racing savvy to compete with Senna – time and again the Brazilian would outperform his French teammate in qualifying (he won a staggering 13 pole positions in the year, compared to just two for Prost), only for Prost to turn the tables in the race. The Frenchman won three of the first four races and then three of the last four to push Senna to the limit.

Ron Dennis, McLaren's team principal, summed up the situation when commenting: "Beating each other became far more challenging than beating the rest of the field." This began to affect Senna's driving, as simply beating Prost was not enough. At Monaco, in the third race of the season, Senna had a comfortable lead with time running out but he kept pushing, despite cautions from his team. He eventually pushed too hard and crashed, handing Prost the victory, but he spoke of entering a "different dimension" with his driving, one beyond ordinary consciousness. That different dimension spurred him to a devastating midseason run of six wins in seven races.

« Senna leads the field at Imola in 1994, before his fatal crash

Victory at Japan, in the penultimate race of the season, would see Senna win his first world title. Disastrously, he stalled in pole position and fell back to 14th, but in the rain he began to work his way back up through the field. Finally, he overtook Prost to secure the win and the championship. If that had seemed like a dramatic finish, it paled in comparison to what followed. The 1989 season would become infamous for a ruling from the FIA that nearly drove Senna out of the sport.

The familiar pattern of Senna dominating in qualifying but struggling in races continued in 1989, as he endured a feast-or-famine season. Out of 16 races he secured pole position 13 times, translating that to six victories, but he failed to finish in five other races. The steadier Prost led the championship as the Japanese Grand Prix rolled around again. By now it was proving difficult for Senna and Prost to coexist. Two strong but contrasting personalities were never going to

get along in such a high-pressure environment, and the competitiveness reached breaking point at Suzuka.

Only a win for Senna would keep the championship alive, and when he saw a narrow gap going into the Casio chicane on lap 46 of 53, he took his chance. Prost appeared to slam the door on Senna, leading to a collision that saw both cars spin off. Crucially, Senna was able to restart his car and rejoin the race. After pitting to have his front wing replaced, he chased down the new leader, Alessandro Nannini, and took the lead at the same chicane that had ended Prost's race. It was a stunning, audacious victory, and it kept the championship alive into the last week... but then the FIA stepped in.

In a shock announcement, Senna was stripped of the win, handing the title to Prost, because he had rejoined the track via the escape road rather than by turning around and going back through the chicane. The absurdity of the charge was made clear by Senna's team, which pointed out that exactly the same thing had happened in previous races with no sanctions being imposed.

Despite this evidence being presented, FIA president Jean-

AFTERMATH OF IMOLA

Senna's was not the only fatality to force Formula 1 to adapt new safety protocols, but it was a seminal moment in the sport. It had been 12 years since a driver had lost his life during a race meeting, and the deaths of Senna and Roland Ratzenberger, as well as the stomach-churning crash survived by Rubens Barrichello, ushered in a new era of safety protocols. A review was initiated, and enhancements to driver safety have been ongoing ever since. It would be 20 years before another driver lost his life, when Jules Bianchi was fatally injured at Suzuka in 2014.

Improving protection and support for the head and neck were priorities after Senna's crash. This continued

in 2003, with the introduction of the Head and Neck Support (HANS) device. A 'survival cell' now cocoons the driver, made of carbon fibre, which is able to resist penetration by flying debris. Wheels are tethered to stop them detaching after impact and medical teams are positioned around tracks to ensure they can reach any point within 30 seconds of an incident. Most striking of all was the introduction, in 2018, of the 'halo', which protects a driver's head from impact.

Along with improvements in track design, drivers are now able to walk away almost unscathed from crashes of greater intensity than that which claimed Senna's life.

Marie Balestre stubbornly stuck to his guns, proceeding to add a $100,000 fine and a suspended six-month ban for the incident that led to the spin-off. Senna was disgusted and believed that Balestre, a Frenchman, was biased towards his countryman, Prost. He briefly contemplated retirement.

The relationship between Prost and Senna was now toxic and the two could not hope to exist in the same team for any longer. Prost left to join Ferrari, but the two exchanged bitter barbs. Senna said of Prost: "All drivers go to their limit. My limit is different from Prost's. That is the reality. And instead of trying to improve his own skills, he found it easier to attack me."

In turn, Prost had this to say about his mercurial rival: "Ayrton has a small problem. He thinks that he can't kill himself because he believes in God... and I think that's very dangerous for the other drivers."

In the end, Senna could not walk away from what he described as, "my aim, my target, my object, my passion, my dream, my life". He would race again the next year.

SECOND DRIVERS' CHAMPIONSHIP

The 1990 season saw Senna and Prost once more fight for the title in a championship that again came down to Japan. The

 Senna pits during a Formula 3 race in 1983

two drivers had engaged in a thrilling season, each putting together devastating sequences of results to take and retake control.

Senna opened with three victories in the first five races, before Prost countered with three straight wins in Mexico, France and Great Britain. Senna responded with three wins in the next four races to build a commanding lead. As the Formula 1 circus moved to Suzuka once more, the situation was eerily similar to that of the preceding season, but this time it was Prost who had to win to keep his hopes alive.

In contrast to the drama of 1989, the 1990 Japanese Grand Prix was something of an anticlimax, but there was still no shortage of controversy. Still feeling that the authorities were against him, Senna had stormed out of a pre-race meeting when a warning against dangerous driving had been read out. Clearly, he felt the warning was aimed squarely at himself, and when alignments on the starting

 Senna, in his JPS Lotus gear, alongside Alain Prost, Nigel Mansell and Nelson Piquet, in 1986

grid were changed, giving Prost (starting in second place) a favourable position on the racing line, Senna again complained angrily.

Sure enough, Prost took advantage of the better grip on his section of the track in order to blow past Senna at the start. In response, Senna attempted to dart through a narrow gap, the cars came together, and both men spun off. The Japanese Grand Prix was over for both of them at the first corner.

Controversy raged over the incident, but replays clearly showed that Prost had moved to his left, offering a narrow gap for Senna to attack. As Senna said succinctly afterwards, in a phrase that summed up his attitude to the sport: "If you no longer go for a gap that exists, you are no longer a racing driver."

It was a somewhat disappointing end to the season. Senna failed to finish in any of the last three races, but he was world champion for the second time.

THE WILLIAMS CHALLENGE

A new threat was emerging as the 1991 season opened. The Williams team had brought back British driver Nigel Mansell and were set to take over the world of F1, but for the time being, Senna managed to hold on to his spot. Winning the first four races from pole position suggested the season might be a stroll for the Brazilian, but as Mansell settled back

🔺 A light moment with Prost after Senna joins McLaren in 1988

into his old team, he mounted a fierce midseason charge that was in fact a warning signal for the following season. Senna held on to win comfortably, finishing 24 points ahead of Mansell to take the title, but it was to be his last world championship.

The following year, with Williams introducing waves of electronic enhancements to their cars, Senna saw his competitiveness eroded. He won pole position just once as Mansell dominated. The Brit won eight of the first ten races and Senna had no doubts why.

"When you go into this sort of electronic war," he commented, "you can find yourself completely stuck. The electronics will do the work and not the driver and I don't think that is what you want." Despite his distaste for the enhancements employed by Williams, Senna recognised them as the team to be with and attempted to switch. Williams, however, had just signed Prost, who made it clear he would not drive alongside Senna again.

The 1993 season was a replay of 1992, with Prost taking Mansell's place and winning 13 pole positions, while teammate Damon Hill won two. Senna fought heroically and

won five races, but Prost could not be caught. Prost's fourth championship triggered his immediate retirement and the way was now open for Senna to join Williams.

It was always a strange pairing – Williams' team principal Frank Williams described Senna as "the best piece of equipment, in a way, you can put in the machine" – but rule changes prior to the 1994 season meant Senna never got to race in the advanced Williams car. The electronic enhancements had to be stripped out, leaving the car difficult to handle. Senna struggled with what was left, and believed that Michael Schumacher, in the Benetton, was benefitting from illegal electronic enhancements. He managed to get his car into pole position for the first three races, but Schumacher was unstoppable on the way to his first championship.

At the same time, the retirement of Prost had robbed Senna of his primary motivation. In a way, he felt lost without the diminutive Frenchman to spar against, and he even phoned his old rival to try and persuade him to come out of retirement. It was the start of an unexpected end to the men's relationship, as intense rivalry started to give way to friendship.

Where this friendship might have led can never be known, because the 1994 season would see Senna's career and life come to a shocking end at Imola, on 1 May. In retrospect, the omens were bad from the start. Rubens Barrichello was seriously injured in a crash during practice, and then Roland Ratzenberger was fatally injured during qualifying. Senna was struggling to settle in with the Williams team, and his personal life was also turbulent, as he fought to get his new girlfriend, Adriane Galisteu, accepted by his family.

On top of this, Senna had warned that it was dangerous to remove the electronic enhancements from F1 cars without curbing their speed, and his words appeared prophetic following the serious crashes that punctuated the weekend at Imola. As the race started, there was a lot on the Brazilian's mind, but he led in the early stages as he took his car into Tamburello corner. The cause of Senna's death after his car crashed at Tamburello remains uncertain, but it appears part of the car's suspension struck his helmet at just the right point to cause a fatal head injury.

Senna's body was flown back to São Paulo on 4 May for his funeral, and Prost was one of his coffin-bearers. The inscription on his grave reads: "Nada pode me separar do amor de Deus", which translates to 'Nothing can separate me from the love of God.'

» Senna, pictured in 1992 during tyre testing for the British Grand Prix at Silverstone

LEGACY

Senna's rivalry with Prost not only produced fireworks on the track, but was hugely beneficial to Formula 1 off the track. The sport enjoyed a surge in popularity as the 1990s opened, fuelled in part by the compelling storylines served up by two of the greatest drivers of all time slugging it out toe-to-toe. On a smaller scale, Senna was also seen as a ray of sunshine, perhaps the only ray of sunshine, during a bleak time for Brazil. A symbol of resilience and dashing bravery, Senna gave Brazilians something to be proud of.

But of course, it is his life on the track that will be remembered most vividly. Senna was a passionate, instinctive driver. Matched against the cool calculations of Prost, he took on the qualities of a matador. Aggressive, driven and always seeking to push himself and his car to the limit, he never found the peace that he claimed to be searching for. In truth, he had probably found it earlier in life, when he raced karts in a sport devoid of politics and money. It was, in his words, "pure driving, pure racing". He never quite found that again.

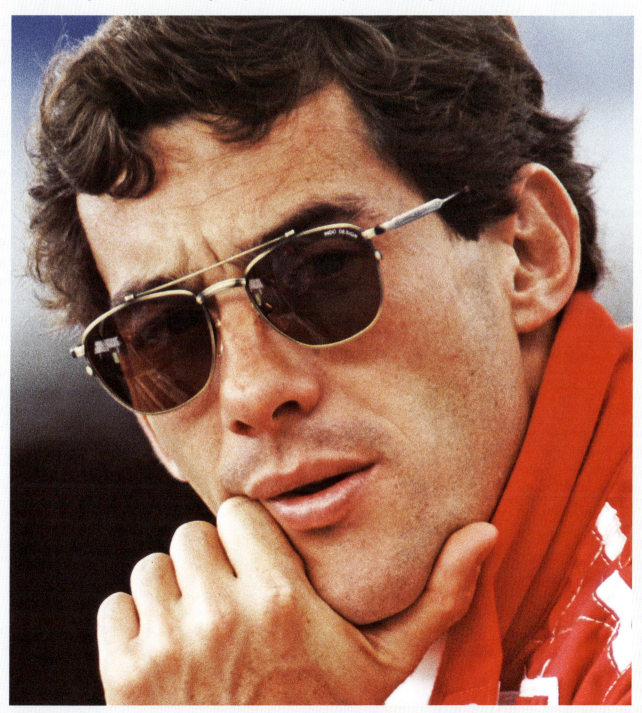

INFO

Nationality
British

Teams
BRM (1965–1967)
Matra (1968–1969)
Tyrrell (1970–1973)

Championships
3 (1969, 1971, 1973)

Number of races
99

Number of race wins
27

Number of podiums
43

Pole positions
17

JACKIE STEWART
THE FLYING SCOT

Jackie Stewart was not only a great champion, he helped usher in a new era of safety consciousness

Many men have achieved immortality through their exploits on a racing circuit, but only a select few have influenced the sport of Formula 1 to the extent that they have actually saved lives. Ayrton Senna's fatal crash at Imola in 1994 turned out to be a heroic sacrifice as it forced the sport to instigate a raft of changes to improve safety. However, it shouldn't be forgotten that Jackie Stewart had laid the foundation for those changes decades earlier. In fact, before Stewart came along, it is not unreasonable to argue that there were no safety standards in Formula 1 at all.

Driving was not the first love of John Young Stewart – that position is held by shooting, at which he excelled, being nearly good enough to represent Great Britain at the Olympics. Once he got behind the wheel of a car, however, there was almost literally no stopping him – he caught the eye of Ken Tyrrell and raced in British Formula 3 in 1963, displaying such dominance that he once won seven consecutive races.

FORMULA 1

Stewart's Formula 1 career began with BRM in 1965, alongside Graham Hill. The season comprised just ten races at the time, with only the six best results counting, and Stewart finished third in the Drivers' Championship despite only managing a single race victory, at the Italian Grand Prix. He won the first race of the following season, but only managed to complete two more races in a disappointing year that saw him finish in seventh place. It was a similar story in 1967, as he failed to finish in nine of the 11 races.

Stewart was on a personal crusade to make the sport safer. At Belgium, in 1966, he had found himself stuck in a ditch with fuel spilling all over him. There were no marshals present and he was lucky that two other drivers had crashed near the same spot. Finally finding his way into an ambulance, the driver got lost on the way to hospital.

⯆ Stewart en route to winning the Spanish Grand Prix in 1971 for Tyrrell

If Stewart's injuries had been more severe than a broken collarbone, the results of such pathetically inadequate safety precautions could have been tragic, and Stewart was determined to instigate changes. His stature as an up-and-coming driver, with two Grand Prix victories under his belt, certainly helped, but he was opposed not only by the authorities, but by some drivers, who felt he was displaying a lack of courage and threatening to take the fun out of the freewheeling sport.

"It was simply ridiculous," he later recalled. "Here was a sport that had serious injury and death so closely associated with it, yet there was no infrastructure to support it, and very few safety measures to prevent it. So, I felt I had to do something."

But the criticism was virulent and personal. "It was said I removed the romance from the sport," he recalled, "that the safety measures took away the swashbuckling spectacular that had been. They said I had no guts."

It seems incredible to think a Formula 1 driver could be accused of having no guts, and equally incredible that seatbelts were not mandatory for drivers before this point. Nor were full-face visors. Stewart campaigned for proper medical teams to be present at all races and for barriers to be installed on sections of the track where cars might spin off. Formula 1 remained a deadly sport even after these fairly modest changes, but it is certain that Stewart's campaigning saved the lives of some of his fellow drivers – perhaps even some of those who had been so opposed to his crusade.

Stewart's car approaches the burning wreckage from a major crash in Spain in 1970

THE CHAMPIONSHIPS

Switching teams in 1968 proved a good move for Stewart. Ken Tyrrell had moved into Formula 1 and his Matra Ford was a car Stewart could compete in. He won three races to finish second, behind Hill. In 1969 he went one better, after winning five of the first six races and six over the course of the season to win his first Drivers' Championship.

As his profile increased, Stewart felt able to take stronger stands in his push for improved safety. The Belgian track at Spa-Francorchamps was particularly fearsome, as well as being the course on which Stewart had come to grief in 1966. Having walked the track in 1969, Stewart did not think it was safe enough to race on and a drivers' boycott erased it from the calendar for that year. It returned in 1970 after minor safety measures were implemented – Formula 1 was still far from safe, but was moving in the right direction.

After a disappointing 1970 season (he failed to finish eight times), he regained the world championship easily in 1971, winning six of the 11 meetings. By now Stewart was an international name, thanks in part to his rockstar looks. He was in demand from media outlets and also raced in the Can-Am (the Canadian-American Challenge Cup). It is estimated that he flew across the Atlantic 186 times in a year that finally saw his health crack under the pressure. A bout of mononucleosis proved he was not invincible off the track, however good he was on it.

Unfortunately, 1972 proved to be another disappointing year. Wins in the last two races could not do anything to overhaul Emerson Fittipaldi, who won comfortably. Despite poor health, Stewart had once more spread himself thin, competing in the European Touring Cars Championship as well as Formula 1.

Stewart's rockstar looks helped establish him as the first superstar of F1

THE FINAL YEAR

Stewart felt that his time at the top of the game was coming to an end. No doubt continuing safety concerns were a part of his decision, and the 1973 season would be his last – his career would wrap up very neatly in the United States, with his 100th Grand Prix. By then, he had won five races, taking his total to 27 and setting a new record.

His final race, however, was not to be. Stewart calculated that 57 fellow drivers had died during his career, some of them close personal friends, but none affected him more than the last, when François Cevert was killed during practice at Watkins Glen in New York.

Stewart drove another lap of the course, passed where his teammate and friend had died, and decided that was enough. He pulled out of the race and his career was over. It would take 14 years before his record for Grand Prix victories was bettered by Alain Prost.

Stewart's love for the sport was as strong as ever, however, and he worked as a commentator, a consultant and even as a team owner. Stewart Grand Prix took to the grid in 1997 and won at the infamous Nürburgring in 1999.

The sport still had a lot of love for Stewart too, even if it had taken time to forgive him for insisting on improved safety standards.

"I would have been a much more popular world champion if I had always said what people wanted to hear," he later mused. "I might have been dead, but definitely more popular."

THE NÜRBURGRING

Perhaps the most notorious of all racetracks, Stewart took immense pride in his four wins at the Nürburgring (as well as securing his only win as a team owner on its tortuous curves). But the track was also an object of dread for the Scotsman.

He remembers: "I won four times at the original Nürburgring in Germany – the most dangerous circuit in the world – and yet I was always afraid of that place. In 1968 I won there by over four minutes in thick fog and rain where you could hardly see the road. That race should never have been held, and having won it by such a big margin gave me more credibility when I demanded safety improvements."

In 1973, Stewart drove and narrated a lap at the Nürburgring with cameras in his car. The shaky footage gives an inkling of the fear the place could instil, but Stewart's words are perhaps even more chilling.

"You're going up here with so much G-forces on," he said at one point on the course, "that you can't take your foot off the throttle and get it onto the brakes."

After his lap he commented: "For a quick lap of the

Nürburgring, you've probably experienced more in seven minutes and six or seven seconds than most people have experienced in all their life in the way of fear and the way of tension and the way of animosity towards machinery and to a racetrack."

Stewart flashes by in the rain at the Nürburgring in 1968

INFO

Nationality
Netherlands

Teams
Toro Rosso (2015–2016)
Red Bull (2016–)

Championships
2 (2021, 2022)

Number of races
163

Number of race wins
35

Number of podiums
77

Pole positions
20

MAX VERSTAPPEN
SUPERMAX

The young gun who pushes to the limit and beyond in his quest for success

Most 17-year-olds struggle with driving lessons and the theory test. Max Verstappen was different. When the 2015 season kicked off in Australia, Verstappen qualified his Toro Rosso in 12th place at the tender age of 17 years and 166 days, beating the record for the youngest driver to start a Grand Prix by nearly two years. Two weeks later he qualified sixth and finished seventh to become the youngest points scorer. Just over a year later, Verstappen won his debut Grand Prix with Red Bull to become the youngest race winner.

The baby-faced assassin soon developed a reputation as a no-holds-barred racer. He demonstrated his bravery by storming around the outside of Nico Rosberg at a very wet 2016 Brazilian Grand Prix and made up for a poor start at the 2019 Austrian Grand Prix by picking off Charles Leclerc's Ferrari with two laps to go, tricking him with a dummy before pouncing on the inside. But Verstappen's aggression often came at a price. Felipe Massa branded Verstappen 'dangerous' after clipping the back of Romain Grosjean in Monaco in 2015, Kimi Räikkönen offered similar criticism in Belgium a year later and Esteban Ocon had an unseemly scuffle with Verstappen at the end of the 2018 Brazilian GP.

But by 2021, Verstappen had earned two third-place finishes in the Drivers' Championship and the F1 world was waiting for him to challenge Lewis Hamilton for the title. And he finally did. He took pole position in Bahrain, the first race of the season. Although Lewis Hamilton slipped by early on, Verstappen didn't give up. On lap 53, just four from the end, he overtook Hamilton but went off track while doing so. Race control ordered him to let Hamilton back past and Verstappen trailed him home in second place.

That Bahrain overtake was the first of many controversial events in a season that saw the fiercest rivalry develop since Senna and Prost. Verstappen and Hamilton traded places at the top of the standings and traded paint on the

« Verstappen was the sixth driver to take a seat at Red Bull after coming through their driver academy and the third to win a Grand Prix

track. Verstappen's clumsy attempt to take the lead on the first lap of the British Grand Prix led to a collision with Hamilton. Although the Brit came out of it unscathed and went on to win the race, Verstappen slid sideways into a gravel trap and collided with a tyre wall at 290 km/h (180 mph). His race weekend ended with him being checked out at a local hospital. In Italy, Hamilton came out of the pits side by side with Verstappen. Neither man backed down as they raced through turns one and two. Verstappen was forced onto a kerb, clipped Hamilton's rear tyre and was launched into the air, landing on top of Hamilton's cockpit. Damage forced both drivers to retire and the post-race investigation deemed Verstappen to be most at fault. Were it not for the newly introduced halo device, the crash could have cost Hamilton far more than a few championship points.

But Verstappen also showed his sheer speed and skill when he had the luxury of driving in clean air without Hamilton around. He took his first grand slam at the Austrian Grand Prix, taking pole position, leading the race from start to finish and setting the fastest lap. And although it seemed he had been around for ages, Verstappen set a new record as the youngest driver to achieve a grand slam.

Ultimately, the Drivers' Championship came down to the final lap of the final race. And, surprise, surprise, there was controversy involved. When a crash brought out the safety car with five laps to go, second-placed Verstappen pitted for fresh tyres. Hamilton did not pit, as it would have sacrificed the lead. But then, race director Michael Masi made two questionable calls. He allowed the five cars between Hamilton and Verstappen to unlap themselves – but only those five. And he insisted there was time for a one-lap run-off. Verstappen used his fresh tyres to overtake and take the title by eight points. Cue wild celebrations in the Low Countries and howls of outrage from Lewis Hamilton fans.

Though the circumstances of that race and the season as a whole were marred by controversy, Verstappen had finally become world champion for the first time. It was a destiny many had expected him to fulfil since watching his teenage debut.

⌃ Verstappen and Hamilton's battle for the 2021 World Championship was one of the most thrilling in recent years

Even if some claim there is an asterisk in the history books next to his first Drivers' Championship title, nobody can deny he was a worthy winner of his second, because Verstappen retained the Drivers' Championship in 2022 by a comfortable margin. Although he suffered two retirements in the first three races as Red Bull struggled with their fuel system, Verstappen benefited from the performance of Hamilton's Mercedes falling off a cliff. Verstappen's main rival in 2022 would be Ferrari's Charles Leclerc, but he was usually a distant challenger.

Verstappen sliced Leclerc's early-season championship lead at the fourth round, the Emilia Romagna Grand Prix, when he scored his second grand slam of flag-to-flag race win, fastest lap and pole position. That was the first of five wins from the next six races; his only failure came when teammate Sergio Pérez kept him off the top step in Monaco.

Then, Verstappen won five in a row between rounds 12 and 16.

The title came his way at the end of the Japanese Grand Prix, when there were still six races to run. And as if to remind F1 watchers that nothing is simple when Verstappen is involved, he was crowned in unusual circumstances. The race started in heavy rain and was red flagged after two laps, with Verstappen retaining the lead from pole. After a long break, the race resumed behind the safety car before it eventually pulled off for a brief period of live racing, but the chequered flag was waved after 28 laps due to the race passing its three-hour time limit. Verstappen returned to the pits thinking he would be awarded half points for winning the shortened race, but the race officials decided that full points were on offer. They then gave Leclerc a five-second penalty for cutting a chicane, dropping him to third place. Verstappen now had an insurmountable 113-point lead in the Drivers' Championship. Once again, he had won the season-long race for points due to a race official's decision.

But he would have won the title had the officials not intervened, because the stats for Verstappen's second championship-winning season were stunning. He won 15

MOTORSPORT IN THE BLOOD

He may be known as the Flying Dutchman, but Max Verstappen was actually born in Hasselt, a city in Belgium near the Dutch border. And his family pedigree ensured there was never a doubt that young Max would be a racer. His mother, Sophie Kumpen, competed successfully in karting. Her cousin, Anthony Kumpen, is a two-time NASCAR Whelen Euro Series champion, and her uncle, Paul Kumpen, is a former motocross and endurance rally driver.

But F1 fans of a certain age will most remember Max's father, Jos Verstappen, who competed in the most prestigious form of motorsport over eight seasons for seven different teams. Jos made his debut in 1994 when he stepped in for the injured JJ Lehto for Benetton. It was an eventful debut – Jos somersaulted his car after being forced onto the grass and grazed the helmet of Martin Brundle in an eerie premonition of the time his son's car would almost make contact with the helmet of Lewis Hamilton. Later that season, fuel leaked onto Verstappen's car during a pitstop and it was briefly engulfed in a fireball. Both times, Jos was unhurt. Jos remained in F1 but changed teams every season for the next five years: to Simtek, Arrows, Tyrrell, Stewart and Honda. He returned to Arrows, before finishing his career with Minardi. He never troubled the F1 podium beyond two consecutive third-place finishes in his season with Benetton, but he is in the relatively exclusive 100-plus Grand Prix club.

Jos and his wife separated when Max was a child, but he coached Max and attended his son's races whenever his own racing schedule allowed. Max chooses to compete with a Dutch racing license because he spent so much time competing in kart races over the border in the Netherlands with his father by his side.

of 22 races with seven pole positions and five fastest laps. It was the most race wins in a single season, breaking the mark of 13 set by Michael Schumacher in 2004 and Sebastian Vettel in 2013. When he didn't win, he finished on the podium in two of the other seven races. That helped him to a total of 454 points, breaking the previous record of 413 set by Lewis Hamilton in 2019. And unlike 2021, when Mercedes were the winning constructor, Verstappen and Pérez combined to give Red Bull a blistering 205-point margin over Ferrari in the Constructors' Championship.

Recent Formula 1 history has tended to run in eras in which one driver dominates. Michael Schumacher was the man in the early 2000s. Then came Sebastian Vettel in the early 2010s, then Lewis Hamilton to end the decade. Are we now seeing another changing of the guard? Few would be surprised if, a decade from now, Verstappen has matched – or even surpassed – his illustrious compatriots.

» Verstappen's father Jos was a journeyman driver who competed in 106 Grand Prix for six different teams

SEBASTIAN VETTEL
THE CHARGING BULL

Sebastian Vettel smashed countless Formula 1 records but couldn't find the finesse at Ferrari

It is said that if you want to build a champion, then you need to start young. This is certainly true of Sebastian Vettel, the man who spent the first half of his Formula 1 career becoming the youngest driver to achieve a whole host of records. Born in Heppenheim, Germany, Vettel's karting career started by the age of three, thanks in no small part to his motorsport-obsessed father Norbert. He was driving competitively by seven and impressed instantly with his skill, fearlessness and fascination with the technical side of the sport. It was this blend of dedication and ability that saw young Vettel rack up multiple wins and trophies, one of which was handed to him by none other than F1 legend and Vettel's personal hero Michael Schumacher. Clearly this was a child destined for greatness.

Long before Red Bull were an active Formula 1 team, they sponsored promising young drivers to help them progress through the motorsport world. Vettel was one of those drivers and, aged 13, was signed up to the Red Bull Junior Team. That clearly helped as Vettel stormed to the 2004 Formula BMW ADAC title, winning 18 of the 20 races. This form attracted the attention of Sauber, for whom Vettel test drove while still a teenager. Then, in 2007, he stood in for Robert Kubica at the United States Grand Prix and drove a masterful race at Indianapolis. Vettel qualified seventh and ended the race eighth. That earned him a debut point, becoming the youngest driver to do so. This clearly impressed Toro Rosso, who were effectively Red Bull's feeder team. Four races later they parachuted the young German into a seat where he struggled initially, finishing near the back of the field in his first four races and recording two consecutive DNFs, before a stunning drive in China saw him finish fourth. He did enough in that half-season to retain his seat the following year and repaid Toro Rosso handsomely. Despite recording four DNFs at the start of the 2008 season, Vettel stunned the world of motorsport by claiming pole at the Italian Grand Prix at Monza and, despite soaking wet conditions, cruising to a dominant win. It was Toro Rosso's first Grand Prix victory and made Vettel both the youngest-ever polesitter and

Vettel's battles with Hamilton are legendary, but this became a common sight during the German's time at Ferrari

youngest-ever winner in the sport. Vettel was suddenly hot property indeed.

His performances in a car that could usually be found near the back of the grid convinced the main Red Bull team to take a punt on him after he outscored veterans Mark Webber and David Coulthard, despite driving the inferior car. He replaced the retiring Coulthard to partner Webber in the exciting Red Bull garage, and what a decision that was.

Red Bull had been mixing it in the midfield since they bought out Jaguar in 2005, but their new star catapulted them to the front of the grid. Vettel's victory in China was the team's first in Formula 1 and he followed it up with wins in Great Britain, Japan and Abu Dhabi. These helped him finish second in the driver standings, 11 points behind surprise champion Jenson Button. Clearly Red Bull and Vettel were a perfect match for each other. The 2010 season saw a major shake-up in the sport with 25 points now given to the race winner to try to encourage drivers to push for the victory, rather than settle for a safe second. This suited the fast and ultra-competitive Vettel down to the ground, as he won in

INFO

Nationality
German

Teams
Sauber (2007)
Toro Rosso (2007-2008)
Red Bull (2009-2014)
Ferrari (2015-2020)
Aston Martin (2021-2022)

Championships
4 (2010, 2011, 2012, 2013)

Number of races
299

Number of race wins
53

Number of podiums
122

Pole positions
57

Malaysia and Europe. It was a five-way battle for the title for much of the season as Vettel and Webber took on Ferrari's two-time champion Fernando Alonso, as well as McLaren's British duo of Button and Lewis Hamilton. It looked like Alonso was going to take his third crown with victory in South Korea, but Vettel won in Brazil to keep the championship alive. Going into the final race in Abu Dhabi, Alonso had an eight-point lead over Webber and a 15-point lead over Vettel, with Hamilton needing an incredible set of results to win the title. Vettel did all he could, leading from pole and cruising to a dominant victory and ending Hamilton's chances of a second title – but what about the men who could deny him a maiden championship? He faced a nervous wait after crossing the line but, with Alonso and Webber finishing seventh and eighth respectively, Vettel was confirmed as the youngest-ever Formula 1 world champion. Remarkably it was the first time he had led the championship all season and he had done it at the age of 23, beating the mark set by Hamilton two years earlier. Vettel was already a history-

❯ Vettel and Schumacher had a long, special relationship – even as the former was stealing the latter's records

making superstar, having defeated a brilliant two-time champion and an experienced teammate to the coveted title – an amazing achievement.

However, he wasn't done there, not by a long shot. Vettel enjoyed a staggeringly dominant season in 2011. He won five of the first six races of the season and then five of the final eight, claiming a second title with an incredible four races still to go – the joint third-fastest win in history. He also became the youngest two-time champion, taking the record off Alonso.

Like Alonso, it looked like Vettel would get stuck on two championships, after a poor start to the 2012 season. He won just one of the opening 13 races of the season, trailed Alonso by a whopping 39 points and was also behind Hamilton and Kimi Räikkönen in the standings. The turning point came in Singapore where he roared to victory, the first of four in a row that catapulted him to the top of the standings. The championship went down to the final race of the season again, but this time it was a straight fight between just Vettel and Alonso. Vettel started fourth with Alonso in seventh at

« Vettel's traditional celebration got an awful lot of use during his time at Red Bull

THE RAGING BULL

As the likes of Schumacher, Hamilton and Verstappen have shown, you need a bit of fire in your belly if you are to achieve greatness in Formula 1. Vettel is no exception and has had a number of notable moments when his will to win took him over the edge. The first sign of this attitude was in 2010 when he tried to overtake teammate Webber and caused a dramatic crash that cost Red Bull victory and knocked him out of the race.

If that wasn't bad enough, in 2013 Webber was leading from Vettel at the Malaysian Grand Prix. Despite team orders telling the pair to hold their positions to guarantee the 1-2, Vettel repeatedly attacked, at one point being told by team principal Christian Horner, "This is silly, Seb. Come on". The German eventually got past and won the race, but ruined his professional relationship with Webber and had to apologise to the furious Australian. Then at Ferrari there was that bizarre incident with Hamilton where he bashed into his rival twice, before another astonishing moment at the 2019 Canadian Grand Prix. Vettel was leading but, under pressure from Hamilton, went onto the grass. In returning to the track he squeezed Hamilton against the wall, which the stewards ruled deserved a five-second penalty. Vettel won the race, but the penalty dropped him to second. Furious at the decision, he swapped over the

first and second-placed boards in the winners enclosure to make his feelings clear. Never one to shirk a challenge or a fight, Vettel truly has the mentality of a champion.

⌃ Vettel leaving no one in any doubt who he thought the real race winner was in Canada in 2019

Reliability issues from both car and driver affected Vettel's time at Ferrari

a wet Interlagos, but it was the worst possible start for the German as he lost places off the line and was then involved in a collision with Bruno Senna, spinning and falling dead last. Undeterred, Vettel fought his way back up the field and was running eighth before too long. Alonso put in a supreme display in awful conditions to get himself into second, but needed Vettel to finish eighth or lower to take the title. It wasn't to be, however, as Vettel squeezed past compatriot and hero Schumacher into sixth and when Paul di Resta's crash brought out the safety car, Vettel just needed to cross the line to become a three-time champion. Aged just 25 he became the youngest triple champion, reaching the mark six years quicker than Ayrton Senna. In winning his third title in a row, Vettel had also taken another age-related record off the man who had inspired him as a youngster, achieving the three-peat eight years quicker than the great Schumacher.

So after three consecutive championship wins, could Vettel make it a fourth? He controversially won in Malaysia after disobeying team orders to stay behind teammate Mark Webber when the Red Bull duo were running first and second, before wins at Bahrain, Canada and Germany saw

him take a 38-point lead over Räikkönen at the summer break. If any of his rivals thought there was a chink in his armour then they were to be sadly mistaken, as in the end it was no contest. Vettel went on an unprecedented nine-race winning streak, taking every single remaining Grand Prix of the season in an unheard-of display of dominance, speed and consistency. From a potentially treacherous position, Vettel had blown away the pack and cantered to the title with three races to spare. That made it four wins on the spin for Vettel, putting him level with Alain Prost and only behind Juan Manuel Fangio and Schumacher. Once again, Vettel was the youngest to four titles by some distance and looked well on his way to matching Schumacher's record of five straight championship titles. However, while no other driver could match his peerless talent, something else got in his way. In a bid to become greener, Formula 1 bosses insisted engines be replaced by hybrid power units, which played right into the hands of the Mercedes team of Hamilton and Nico Rosberg. The pair won 16 of the 19 races, ending Red Bull's stranglehold on the championship and Vettel's four-year reign as champion. The only non-Mercedes driver to win a race was a Red Bull driver, but it wasn't the four-time champion. Webber had retired, leaving a space for his fellow Australian Daniel Ricciardo. The ever-smiling, popular and quick Ricciardo won in Canada, Hungary and Belgium, finishing third in the driver standings, two places above Vettel who failed to win a single race and made the podium just four times.

Vettel wasn't used to not winning. 2014 was just the second time in his career, and the first since his rookie season, in which he'd failed to take the chequered flag. He was unhappy at Red Bull, who had failed to give him a car in which he felt comfortable, and the emergence of exciting young talent Ricciardo mimicked Vettel's own blockbuster entrance to F1 where he usurped established team leader Webber. This prompted him to shock the world of motorsport and seek a new challenge away from the team that had delivered him four consecutive world titles. He found it in the form of the most glamorous team in F1. Ferrari and Alonso had had a fractious relationship, with Scuderia unable to provide a car worthy of the two-time champion's talents. Alonso and Ferrari parted ways and in slid Vettel to the Prancing Horse's stable, looking to emulate his idol Schumacher. Things looked promising, with Vettel winning the second race of the season in Malaysia, but once again the field was blown away by the dominance of Mercedes. Vettel was well behind the duo of Hamilton and Rosberg, but miles ahead of the rest of the field and the partnership with Ferrari showed promising signs. However, the 2016 season was a disaster. Vettel failed to win a race for the second time in three seasons, with driver errors and team failures costing him several opportunities to take a Grand Prix. To make matters worse, he finished behind the Red Bull of Ricciardo and just about edged out young upstart Max Verstappen, a teenager who would eventually take some of Vettel's records.

Things had to get better and in 2017 they did. He won two of the first three races of the season after Ferrari delivered a car many considered to be the best on the grid. His running battle with Hamilton was one for the ages, the championship lead swapping on a regular basis. The pair clashed more than once, banging wheels in Spain before another incident in Azerbaijan. With the race behind a safety car, Vettel ran into Hamilton from behind, then drew alongside him and swerved into the Brit. Vettel initially blamed Hamilton for the incident, before taking responsibility. More engine problems and collisions for Vettel meant that Hamilton won the title with a couple of races to spare, but he was left with a sense of what might have been were it not for reliability issues and his own temper.

That was to prove to be the closest Vettel got to a title in the red of Ferrari. He wasn't able to mount any kind of challenge to Hamilton the following season, despite again

having one of the best cars on the grid. The following two seasons were disasters, finishing behind yet another young, exciting new teammate in Charles Leclerc. Just as he had done at Red Bull, with an uncompetitive car and a new kid on the block, Vettel moved teams, this time to Aston Martin. He and teammate Lance Stroll were perennial midfielders, but Vettel did manage two podiums. He should have earned a maiden win for his new team in Hungary after a superb drive, but devastatingly had insufficient fuel left at the end of the race for testing and was disqualified.

There will always be question marks around Vettel's career. Is he an all-time great, or did he just happen to be in the right car at the right time? It can certainly be argued that every time he has been challenged, either by a rival or a teammate, he has appeared to come up short and jumped ship. Often, in the heat of battle, he came off second best and it was only when he was leading pole to flag that he shone. However, it cannot be denied that as a leader, as a driver and as a competitor he is right up there with the best. No one breaks the records of Alonso, Senna and Schumacher without being an exceptionally talented driver. While it is true that he might have been in the right place at the right time, Vettel sure made his time in the hot seat count.

▶ Vettel after winning his fourth consecutive Formula 1 world championship in 2013

TOP 50
FORMULA ONE
DRIVERS
OF ALL TIME

Count down the truly talented and most memorable to have taken to the track in a Formula 1 racing car

From the birth of the FIA World Championship in 1950 at the British Grand Prix to the final round of the 2022 championship in Abu Dhabi, 772 drivers from 41 different countries have taken to the track in a Formula 1 racing car.

Some did not make it through qualifying to start a race, others have started more than 300. No fewer than 113 drivers have passed the chequered flag to win a Grand Prix, 34 of whom have gone on to take the coveted Drivers' Championship. But are statistics the only way to separate the best from the rest? Is it possible to compare modern drivers to those of an earlier era when seasons were shorter but races were longer? What about those drivers who raced in more dangerous times and lost the chance to complete their careers due to injury or death? This is our attempt to crown the greatest of all time. From multiple world champions to those who just missed out on glory, from drivers with long careers to those who lived fast and died young, join our countdown of the bravest, fastest and most successful men who have jumped behind the wheel of an F1 car.

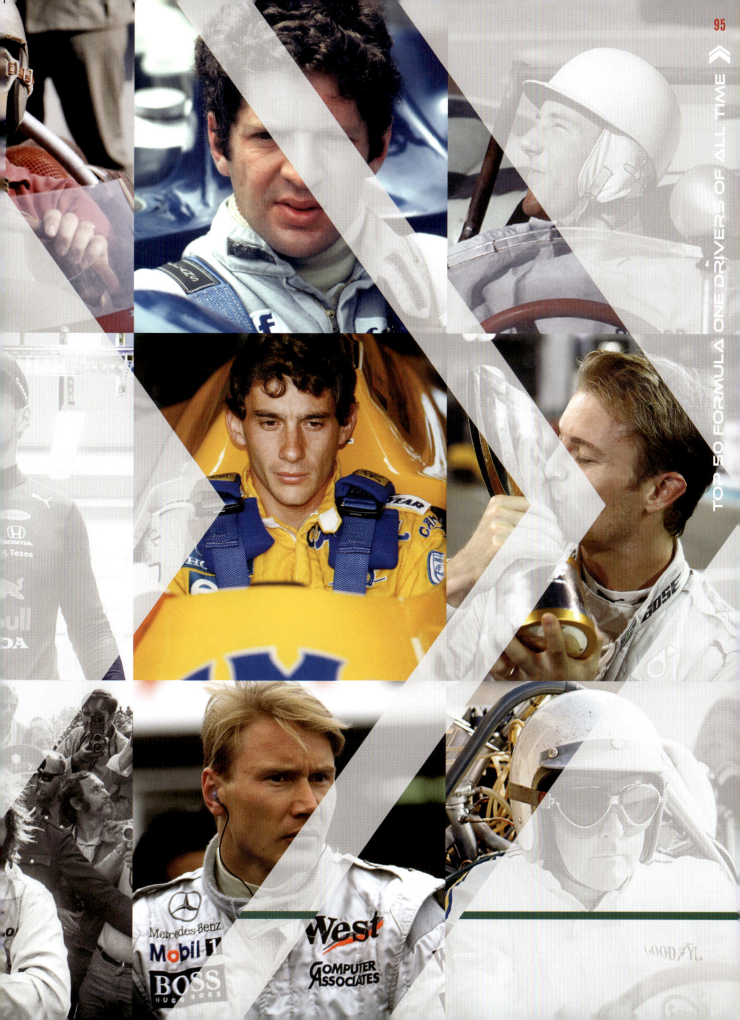

50 CHRIS AMON
1963–1976

In a career spanning 96 races over 14 seasons, Chris Amon never enjoyed the feeling of passing the chequered flag first, although he did win two non-championship races. Nevertheless, he was a talented driver who earned five pole positions and stood on the podium 11 times – he just lacked the stroke of luck needed to reach the top step.

49 FELIPE MASSA
2002, 2004–2017

Felipe Massa thought he was world champion for 30 seconds. He reckoned he had done enough by taking the chequered flag in the final race of the 2008 season, only to see Lewis Hamilton pass Timo Glock on the final corner to finish fifth and take the Drivers' Championship by a solitary point. It remained the highest finish of Massa's 15-year career.

48 DAN GURNEY
1959–1968, 1970

In a long career that saw him win four Grands Prix as well as NASCAR races and the 24 Hours of Le Mans, Dan Gurney was a pioneer. He was the first to wear a full-face helmet and he also began a tradition that lives on in motorsport today – he was the first to spray champagne on the podium after winning.

47 FRANÇOIS CEVERT
1970–1973

A loyal understudy to Jackie Stewart at Tyrrell, François Cevert earned six second-place finishes in 1973 and was due to become team leader when Stewart retired at the end of the year. He never got the chance. Cevert crashed heavily and was instantly killed during qualifying for the final Grand Prix of the season.

46 GERHARD BERGER
1984–1997

Gerhard Berger scored the first and final wins for the Benetton F1 team and in the ten years between, he represented Ferrari and McLaren, with Nigel Mansell and Ayrton Senna among his teammates. Experienced, popular and a consistent performer, it's little surprise that Berger was sought-after by team managers wanting a reliable number two.

44 DAVID COULTHARD
1994–2008

As the Williams test driver, David Coulthard was given Ayrton Senna's seat after his fatal crash at Imola. Coulthard was rarely off the grid for the next 16 years, driving for Williams, McLaren and Red Bull and taking 13 wins. He finished third in the Drivers' Championship on four occasions and was second in 2001 to a dominant Michael Schumacher.

43 TONY BROOKS
1956–1961

The 1957 British Grand Prix was notable as the first time a British constructor won a championship Grand Prix. It was also a shared drive. Tony Brooks piloted the Vanwall car for 26 laps, Stirling Moss took over for the next 64. The victory was one of six in Brooks' career and he went on to finish second in the 1959 Drivers' Championship.

45 RICARDO RODRÍGUEZ
1961–1962

One of a pair of Mexican brothers who raced F1, Ricardo Rodríguez was a rising talent and the then-youngest driver to compete in F1 on his debut. He showed immediate promise by qualifying second in his first Grand Prix but his career ended far too soon, killed in a non-championship Grand Prix in his home country.

42 RUBENS BARRICHELLO
1993–2011

Six-time winner of the Constructors' Championship, each time racing in a supporting role to a teammate who took the Drivers' Championship, Rubens Barrichello perfected the role of number two in a race career that encompassed 322 races in 19 years and resulted in 11 wins and 68 podiums.

❰❰ 41 WOLFGANG VON TRIPS
1956–1961

Wolfgang von Trips was a championship contender in 1961 when he scored two wins and two seconds over the first six races of the season. However, a horror crash at the penultimate race of the season saw the German flung from his car. He was carried from the track dead, as were 15 spectators.

⌃ 40 KEKE ROSBERG
1978–1986

After several years as an also-ran in uncompetitive cars, Keke Rosberg was given a shot at the big time with Williams when Alan Jones announced his surprise retirement. Rosberg immediately took advantage of the situation, winning the 1982 Drivers' Championship despite only winning one race, thanks in part to Didier Pironi's injury-enforced absence.

❰❰ 39 JOHN SURTEES
1960–1972

By winning the 1964 Drivers' Championship, John Surtees became the only world champion on two and four wheels. Equally adept on a bike and in a car, Surtees' only weakness was his hot-headed temper. An argument with Ferrari's team manager led to him quitting the Prancing Horse in 1966 and he spent the rest of his career in uncompetitive cars.

"SURTEES' ONLY WEAKNESS WAS HIS TEMPER"

38 JACKY ICKX
1966–1979

A superb all-rounder who won the 24 Hours of Le Mans six times and the Paris Dakar Rally, Jacky Ickx spent 14 years in F1 with a number of different teams. His best seasons were two consecutive second-place finishes in the Drivers' Championship, in 1969 for Brabham and in 1970 for Ferrari.

37 JACQUES VILLENEUVE
1996–2006

Though some claimed that Jacques Villeneuve was given a seat in a competitive car only by virtue of his famous surname, the colourful and opinionated Canadian repaid Williams' faith in him by finishing second in the Drivers' Championship in his debut season. The following year he went one better and won the title after a somewhat tempestuous battle with Schumacher.

36 JENSON BUTTON
2000–2017

Jenson Button's unspectacular career in F1 seemed at an end when Honda suddenly withdrew from F1 before the 2009 season. He was retained when Ross Brawn bought the team and Button stormed to six wins in the first seven races of the season, leading Brawn to the Constructors' Championship and earning himself a surprise Drivers' Championship.

35 DIDIER PIRONI
1978–1982

Didier Pironi was surely about to become France's first world champion when his Ferrari team arrived at Hockenheim for the 1982 German Grand Prix. He had won two races so far, including a controversial finish when he pipped teammate Gilles Villeneuve to the flag in San Marino, and had a 39-point lead in the Drivers' Championship. However, he attempted to overtake in bad weather during practice and smashed into the back of Alain Prost's Renault. Severe leg fractures meant Pironi never raced Formula 1 again.

34 PHIL HILL
1958–1964, 1966

Phil Hill was a bundle of nerves on the grid before a race, perhaps no surprise considering he was only called up to Ferrari's F1 team in 1958 due to the deaths of Luigi Musso and Peter Collins. He was a careful and cautious driver, meaning his cars suffered relatively few mechanical problems, yet he still carried enough speed to win three Grand Prix. The last was a bittersweet victory. Hill went to the 1961 Italian Grand Prix competing with his teammate von Trips for the Drivers' title, but the German was killed on track. Hill won the title by a solitary point, four days later he was pallbearer at his friend's funeral.

33 DENNY HULME
1965–1974

Nicknamed 'the Bear' due to his gruff, publicity-shy nature, Denny Hulme was nonetheless thrust into the spotlight when he became world champion in 1967. The title went down to the final race of the season and Hulme prevailed over his teammate and team owner, Jack Brabham. The following year, now behind the wheel of a McLaren, Hulme was part of another final race shootout – this time he ended the championship in third place behind Graham Hill and Jackie Stewart. The ever-reliable Hulme finished third again in 1972 but chose to bow out in 1974, having witnessed the deaths of several teammates and rivals over the previous ten years. He scored eight wins in 112 starts.

32 MAX VERSTAPPEN
2015–PRESENT

The youngest driver to have started a Grand Prix was tipped by many to be the youngest ever world champion when he was given a competitive seat at Red Bull in 2016. He didn't manage to achieve that record, mainly thanks to Hamilton, but Max Verstappen did manage to eventually take the title in 2021 after a combative campaign that saw him clash with Hamilton and be hauled in front of the stewards a number of times. Still, Verstappen had the last laugh when he overtook Hamilton on a controversial final lap of the final Grand Prix to take the race win and the championship title.

31 CARLOS REUTEMANN
1972–1982

Carlos Reutemann's talent was obvious from the start when he earned pole position in his first Grand Prix. He finished third in the Drivers' Championship for three different teams – Brabham, Ferrari and Williams – but his best season came in 1981 when he missed out on the title by a single point, his campaign hamstrung by infighting with Williams' teammate Alan Jones, who offered little support on the track. Reutemann started the last race of the season with a one-point lead over Nelson Piquet and on pole position but drifted back to finish eighth, allowing the fifth-placed Brazilian to snatch the glory.

30 JODY SCHECKTER
1972–1980

Jody Scheckter had an inauspicious start to his F1 career. He crashed into Emerson Fittipaldi in his third Grand Prix and caused a pile-up in the next race which led to 11 cars retiring. Only after viewing the horrific aftermath of Cevert's fatal crash did Scheckter rein in his aggressive style. It paid off. The new-look Scheckter scored his first podiums and race wins in 1974, finishing third in the Drivers' Championship. He repeated that achievement in 1976 and finished second in 1977 before finally reaching the top step in 1979. Scheckter was Ferrari's final world champion before a 21-year drought began.

29 ALAN JONES
1975–1981, 1983, 1985–1986

A gritty, straight-talking Australian who took no prisoners, Alan Jones was initially a journeyman racer who made up the numbers with smaller teams before seemingly getting his break at Ferrari for 1978. When that offer fell through – Ferrari turned to Gilles Villeneuve instead – Jones hooked up with Williams, then beginning their second season in F1. It was a great partnership: a no-nonsense driver with a no-nonsense team. Four wins in five races at the tail end of 1979 showed that Jones would be the man to beat in 1980 and he was, winning five races to take the Drivers' Championship title.

28 NICO ROSBERG
2006–2016

Nico Rosberg began his F1 career with Williams, the team his dad Keke won the Drivers' title with in 1982, but it quickly became apparent the son needed to move to a more competitive team. That materialised in 2010 when Rosberg was paired with Schumacher in the inaugural campaign of Mercedes F1. He outscored his illustrious teammate in all three of their seasons together before being paired with Hamilton. Their once-friendly relationship soured as Mercedes allowed the two to compete against each other, and although Rosberg finished second to Hamilton in the Drivers' Championship in 2014 and 2015, he triumphed in 2016.

27 RONNIE PETERSON
1970–1978

While switching between March and Lotus – Ronnie Peterson had two stints with both teams – and spending a year driving a six-wheel Tyrrell in 1977, Peterson amassed ten wins in 123 starts, including second place in the 1971 Drivers' Championship. He earned another second place in 1978 but sadly did not live to enjoy the latter success. During a pile-up on the opening lap of the Italian Grand Prix, Peterson's Lotus was shunted into the barriers and caught fire. Though he was pulled from the wreckage by his fellow drivers with only minor burns, around 27 leg and foot fractures caused fat to build up in his blood stream. The 'Super Swede' died the next day as his kidneys were overwhelmed.

26 JAMES HUNT
1973–1979

'Hunt the Shunt' was as wild off the track as he was on it and found a natural home with Hesketh. The team with an eccentric playboy owner and erratic playboy driver were initially the joke of the grid until Hunt won the 1975 Dutch Grand Prix and ended the season fourth in the standings. When Hesketh closed down at the end of that season, Hunt found a better seat at McLaren and won enough races during the second half of the season to pip Niki Lauda to the Drivers' Championship after the German's near-fatal crash caused him to miss two races.

25 MIKE HAWTHORN
1952–1958

A flamboyant extrovert who often raced wearing a tie, Mike Hawthorn was big, blond and beautiful. He scored two wins and several podiums for Ferrari during the first three years of his F1 career before returning to the Prancing Horse after two years away. He topped the Drivers' Championship in 1958 despite only winning one race – five second places propelled him to the title – but chose to retire early having been ground down by the fatal crashes he witnessed (and in the case of the infamous 1955 Le Mans disaster, was accused of causing). Hawthorn died in a road traffic accident in January 1959, only three months after becoming world champion.

24 MARIO ANDRETTI
1968–1972, 1974–1982

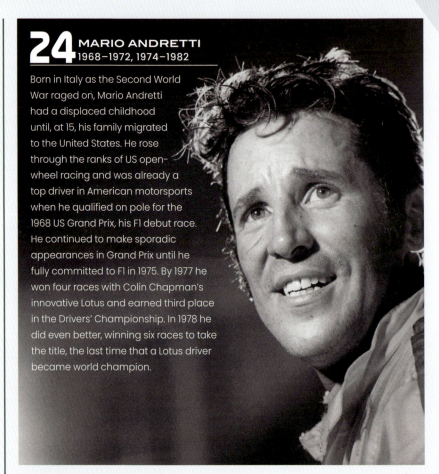

Born in Italy as the Second World War raged on, Mario Andretti had a displaced childhood until, at 15, his family migrated to the United States. He rose through the ranks of US open-wheel racing and was already a top driver in American motorsports when he qualified on pole for the 1968 US Grand Prix, his F1 debut race. He continued to make sporadic appearances in Grand Prix until he fully committed to F1 in 1975. By 1977 he won four races with Colin Chapman's innovative Lotus and earned third place in the Drivers' Championship. In 1978 he did even better, winning six races to take the title, the last time that a Lotus driver became world champion.

23 JOCHEN RINDT
1964–1970

Fast and aggressive on the track, headstrong and abrasive off it, Jochen Rindt always had the potential to win the Drivers' Championship – but he also had the potential to lose his life during a dangerous era. Rindt's Lotus won five out of six races in 1970 before mechanical failure caused him to hit a guardrail in practice for the Italian Grand Prix. The barriers failed to stop his car and Rindt's seatbelt left him with fatal injuries. Although there were still four Grand Prix to run, Ickx could not catch Rindt's points total and he became F1's only posthumous world champion.

22 GILLES VILLENEUVE
1977–1982

Few drivers came into F1 from such an unconventional background – Gilles Villeneuve was a snowmobile racer – and it showed. He was the king of controlling his car at the limit, happy to let it powerslide while engaging opposite lock. He won his first race at the end of his first full season with Ferrari before winning another three, with four second places, to finish second to teammate Scheckter in the 1979 Drivers' Championship. After a couple of years in unusually slow Ferraris, a collision with a coasting car during qualifying at the 1982 Belgian Grand Prix led to Villeneuve's death, his car launched airborne before disintegrating. It was a tragic end for one of the most talented drivers the sport has known.

21 KIMI RÄIKKÖNEN
2001–2009, 2012–2021

When Kimi Räikkönen left McLaren for Ferrari for the 2007 season, it set the scene for a stunning climax to that year's championship. Räikkönen went to the final Grand Prix in third place behind his McLaren replacements Fernando Alonso and Lewis Hamilton, but still in with a slim chance of winning the title. Räikkönen won the race while Alonso and Hamilton could only manage third and seventh, meaning Räikkönen upset the bookmakers to become the new world champion. Two second-place finishes and three third-place finishes in the Drivers' Championship made for a decent haul over his long career – Räikkönen retired in 2021 with more Grand Prix starts than any other driver (349).

20 DAMON HILL
1992–1999

Damon Hill was a late starter to F1. He was 32 when he earned his first drive with Brabham and his time with the purple backmarkers was a disaster – he qualified only twice in eight attempts. Still, two years testing with Williams meant he was given the spare seat in 1993 after Riccardo Patrese retired. He backed up Prost for a year, then shadowed Senna for a few races until the Brazilian's fatal accident. Now, Hill was thrust into the role of team leader. He battled with Schumacher, twice finishing second in the Drivers' Championship behind the German. The 1994 campaign ended with a controversial collision between the two in the last Grand Prix – who was to blame is still debated. Hill made history in 1996 when he became the first child of a world champion to win his own title after taking victory in eight of 16 races, although the new champion was unceremoniously dumped by his team in favour of Heinz-Harald Frentzen.

19 GIUSEPPE FARINA
1950–1956

When the FIA organised the pre-existing series of Grand Prix races into the first official World Championship in 1950, it was 43-year-old Giuseppe Farina who took the chequered flag and set the fastest lap in the first race, the British Grand Prix at Silverstone. He drove his Alfa Romeo to two more wins in the seven-race season to become the inaugural world champion. His straight-back, arms-outstretched driving style was copied by many, although his fellow drivers knew not to go wheel-to-wheel with the ruthless Italian after two drivers died in pre-war collisions with Farina. He was as hard on his machinery as he was on his rivals – Farina's cars often spun or crashed – but the sheer bravery and determination Farina displayed (he even took the lead in the 1954 Belgian Grand Prix despite racing with an arm in plaster) was enough to put him in the record books as the first F1 champion.

17 STIRLING MOSS
1951–1961

The greatest driver never to have become world champion, Stirling Moss came tantalisingly close on many occasions. From 1955 he finished second on four consecutive occasions, the three years after that he finished third. The first British driver to win his home Grand Prix when he crossed the line ahead of Mercedes teammate Juan Manuel Fangio, Moss would eventually end with 16 victories to his name. Prepared to race for works teams or privateers, Moss won races while driving cars made by Mercedes, Maserati, Vanwall, Cooper and Lotus. He much preferred winning in a British marque, though, and was ecstatic when he shared driving duties with Tony Brooks to win the 1957 British Grand Prix, the first victory for a British constructor. He also drove a mid-engine Cooper to the chequered flag in Portugal in 1958, proving that the innovative British design could take on and beat the more established Italian and German teams.

18 NIGEL MANSELL
1980–1992, 1994–1995

It was win or bust for Nigel Mansell. He started 187 races during his 15-year career, winning 31 and crashing out in 32. He hit his prime in 1985 after joining Williams, winning his first Grand Prix at Brands Hatch and shedding a tear on the podium in relief that his long wait had finally ended. Then he couldn't stop winning. He won five races in 1986 and six in 1987, both times finishing second in the Drivers' Championship. A burst tyre in the finale in 1986 gave the title to Prost while a back injury in 1987 caused him to miss a race and handed the title to his fierce rival and teammate, Nelson Piquet. He finished second again in 1991 before finally ascending to the top step in a dominant 1992, having won eight of the first ten races. His career total of 31 race wins leaves him seventh in the all-time list.

16 MIKA HÄKKINEN
1991–2001

A talented driver whose career started slowly before troubling the frontrunners, Mika Häkkinen was coming to the end of his fifth season in F1 when his McLaren ran over debris in qualifying for the 1995 Australian Grand Prix and his car slammed into the wall at sickening speed. A trackside tracheostomy saved his life and Häkkinen returned to continue his slow ascent to the top. He won his first Grand Prix in the final race of 1997 – helped by Coulthard and Jacques Villeneuve moving aside for him – but needed no charity in the season that followed. Häkkinen won eight races en route to a century of points and his first Drivers' Championship; he retained the title ahead of Eddie Irvine in 1999. The quiet Finn bowed out of F1 two years later, having amassed 20 wins in 11 years, all in the second half of his career.

15 EMERSON FITTIPALDI
1970–1980

Emerson Fittipaldi was thrust into the limelight in tragic circumstances. Initially racing a third Lotus to give him experience, Fittipaldi was suddenly his team's number one after Rindt was killed and his other teammate, John Miles, chose to retire in the aftermath. He didn't let the pressure get to him. Fittipaldi immediately stepped up, winning the US Grand Prix and helping to ensure that Rindt won his posthumous title. Two years later, Fittipaldi won five of 12 races to become the then-youngest F1 world champion at the age of 25. After starting strong in the defence of his title in 1973, Fittipaldi's lead was cut and overtaken by Jackie Stewart. A move to McLaren helped Fittipaldi win the title again in 1974 before finishing runner-up in 1975. More titles could have followed for this smooth, calm driver had he not decided to join his brother's also-ran F1 team for the final five years of his career.

13 FERNANDO ALONSO
2001–2018, 2021–PRESENT

In more than 300 races spread over 19 years and five different teams, Fernando Alonso has scored 32 race wins, nearly 2,000 points and two Drivers' Championships. His strength is his consistency. Being equally at home on all types of circuit in all types of weather conditions, means there are few weaknesses that opponents can exploit. His first title came in 2005, early in his career, when Alonso's Renault scored points in all but two of 19 races. The highlight was a superb defensive drive to keep Schumacher at bay in the San Marino Grand Prix, giving Alonso one of his seven wins that year. The following year, Alonso won another seven races and took seven second-place finishes to become a double world champion. Although he hasn't ascended to such heights since, he finished third in the Drivers' Championship for McLaren in 2007 and added three second-place finishes with Ferrari in the first half of the 2010s.

14 GRAHAM HILL
1958–1975

Winner of the Drivers' Championship on two occasions, in 1962 and 1968, and runner-up three times, Graham Hill is the only person to have completed the Triple Crown of Motorsport by winning the Monaco Grand Prix (five times), the Indy 500 and the 24 Hours of Le Mans. Hill's most successful period came in his years with BRM, a team whose fortunes he helped turn around. It was in BRM's colours that Hill won his first Drivers' title, he was also a close contender over the next three years. However, his greatest triumph came in 1968 when he became world champion for a second time. Leading a Lotus team grieving the loss of Jim Clark after an early-season crash, Hill took a car that was fast but unpredictable after the addition of aerodynamic wings and steered it to victory at the final Grand Prix of the season to take the title.

12 ALBERTO ASCARI
1950–1955

The first multiple world champion, Alberto Ascari took the title in 1952 and 1953 and is the only Italian to have won the championship in Ferrari red. Unlike many of his contemporaries, Ascari was cautious and precise, but that did not hold him back. He won six races in 1952 and held the lead for an amazing 304 consecutive laps over five different Grands Prix. The following year he was almost as dominant, this time scoring five wins and a fourth place. Ascari was a superstitious man, perhaps the result of his father dying in the 1925 French Grand Prix, so it is a tragic irony that Ascari died in a Ferrari test session in May 1955, having borrowed a helmet since he left his lucky blue one at home. Even odder, both he and his father were 36 and had won 13 Grand Prix when they died, and both died four days after surviving other crashes.

11 NELSON PIQUET SR
1978–1991

Many F1 drivers found out the hard way that it was a mistake to rule out Nelson Piquet. A master of winning when other drivers were more favoured, Piquet took the leadership of the Brabham team when Lauda retired and helped transform Bernie Ecclestone's outfit into a championship contender. He snatched the Drivers' Championship from Carlos Reutemann at the final race of the 1981 season, which he repeated two years later, this time stealing the trophy from Prost. Piquet enjoyed earning money but Ecclestone enjoyed holding onto it just as much, so Piquet boosted his salary when he became a high-profile signing for Williams. He soon clashed with his new teammate Mansell, but still did enough to earn a third Drivers' Championship in 1987, this time a relatively comfortable victory after Mansell sustained an injury in the penultimate race. To have won three titles in an era when Lauda, Senna, Prost and Mansell were racing illustrates just how talented Piquet was.

09 SEBASTIAN VETTEL
2007–2022

The most successful graduate of Red Bull's driver development programme, Sebastian Vettel served his apprenticeship at Toro Rosso for 18 months before being promoted to Red Bull. It immediately paid dividends. Vettel outscored his more experienced teammate Mark Webber and finished second in the Drivers' Championship before going on an amazing run of four consecutive titles between 2010 and 2013. The first and third of those went down to the final race, but Vettel was untouchable in 2011 and 2013, becoming world champion by more than 100 points each time and winning nine races on the bounce – an F1 record – to finish 2013. Vettel then moved to Ferrari, hoping to emulate the success his countryman Schumacher had there. Unfortunately, 'Baby Schumi' found himself on the losing end of battles with Hamilton in 2017 and 2018. Even so, he still managed to pick up enough race wins to leave him third in the all-time list before moving to Alfa Romeo for 2021.

10 JACK BRABHAM
1955–1970

As happy with his head under the bonnet as he was behind the wheel, Jack Brabham was the ultimate combination of driver and mechanic. His first championship came in a small, mid-engined Cooper in 1959, a car specifically developed to leapfrog the front-engined German and Italian teams. The season culminated in Brabham pushing his car over the line in the final race after running out of petrol. It wasn't such a close-run thing when he retained the title in 1960; Brabham won five consecutive races to ease clear of the field. Two years later, Brabham took the plunge and formed his own team. Brabham's cars became steadily more competitive until, in 1966, he won four races on the trot to take the Drivers' Championship. It remains the only time a driver built his own championship-winning car. He finished second to teammate Hulme in 1967 but could console himself in the knowledge that he had won the Constructors' Championship for the second year in a row.

08 JIM CLARK
1960–1968

Jim Clark duelled with Surtees, Graham Hill and fellow Scotsman Jackie Stewart during the British-dominated racing scene of the 1960s, yet still managed to amass more Grand Prix wins and pole positions than any other driver before his untimely death at the wheel during a Formula 2 race. His talent was initially spotted by Colin Chapman at a ten-lap race at Brands Hatch and the Lotus boss quickly recruited him to his racing team. Clark went on to win the Drivers' Championship for the first time in a peerless 1963 campaign that saw him win a phenomenal seven of ten races, he captured a second title in 1965 and was only prevented from adding more in 1962 and 1964 by engine failure in the last race of the season. A quiet, shy man in a grid of confident extroverts, Clark was nevertheless able to calmly assume control of his Lotus, often coming into his own when faced with difficult driving conditions.

07 JACKIE STEWART
1965–1973

When Ken Tyrrell decided to dip his toe into Formula 1, he immediately formed a partnership with the Scot who would become his greatest driver. Jackie Stewart had been racing with BRM for three years, finishing second in the Drivers' Championship in his debut season, and he matched that achievement in his first year with Tyrrell. He then powered to an easy victory in 1969, winning six of 11 races, and added two more championship titles in 1971 and 1973. Seeing several friends killed in accidents made Stewart a tireless campaigner to improve safety at tracks, pushing for the adoption of safety barriers, seatbelts, run-off areas and full-face helmets. Stewart chose not to compete at his final Grand Prix after the death of his teammate François Cevert in qualifying. He retired not just a treble world champion but a crusader who left the sport in a better condition than it was when he started.

05 NIKI LAUDA
1971–1979, 1982–1985

Few came to F1 more determined than Niki Lauda. He bought his way into drives with March and BRM that threatened to leave him bankrupt and only rewarded him with one finish in the points in three years, but Enzo Ferrari must have seen something in him. He gave Lauda a seat for 1974 and his new driver was challenging for the championship before a string of five retirements at the end of the season ended his chances. A year later, Lauda had transformed the car he initially described as "a piece of shit" into a consistent finisher. He completed all but one race and won the Drivers' Championship. While on course to comfortably defend the title in 1976, a horror crash almost ended Lauda's life. Hauled out of the burning wreckage and administered the last rites by a priest, Lauda rallied and was back on the grid just six weeks later. Only when Lauda considered it too dangerous to race in rain-hit Japan was James Hunt confirmed as the new world champion. The greatest comeback of all time was completed when Lauda took the trophy in 1977, winning the title despite falling out with Ferrari and not attending the final two races. He won it a third time in 1984 behind the wheel of a McLaren.

06 ALAIN PROST
1980–1991, 1993

Known for a smooth and relaxed style that conserved his tyres and allowed him to make a charge late in the race, Alain Prost won four Drivers' Championships, three of which came during a spectacular six-year spell with McLaren. He added four second-place finishes in the championship too. Probably best known for his fierce rivalry with Senna – Prost's teammate at McLaren for two tumultuous seasons – the two clashed on and off the track, including a collision in the penultimate Grand Prix of 1989 that ensured the title went to Prost. Despite an intellectual approach to racing that earned him the nickname of 'the Professor', Prost displayed a degree of pig-headedness that saw him leave teams in acrimonious circumstances on four occasions. Yet it was an indication of his talent that he continued to be given seats in competitive cars, including a final-season drive for Williams that saw him take his fourth Drivers' Championship with seven wins in 16 races.

04 AYRTON SENNA
1984–1994

A genius behind the wheel who drove like a man possessed, Ayrton Senna sought to shave every tiny fraction of a second he could off his lap times. He finished a sensational second to Prost at Monaco in his debut season, despite driving an uncompetitive Toleman and comfortably outperformed three different teammates who tried to keep up with him at Lotus. Senna joined Prost at McLaren in 1988 and won the Drivers' Championship in a season when the McLaren drivers shared every race win between them except one. However, the two drivers were more rivals than teammates. Prost hit Senna in the 1989 Japanese Grand Prix, a collision that meant the Frenchman finished top of the standings. Senna returned the favour in 1990, ensuring he won the Drivers' Championship by taking out Prost at the first corner. He defended the title in 1991 in a campaign largely free of controversy that confirmed Senna as the sport's number one, although three titles seem too few for such a brilliant driver. Perhaps there would have been more, but Senna died at the 1994 San Marino Grand Prix, his third race for Williams, after his car left the track and speared the crash barrier.

03 JUAN MANUEL FANGIO
1950–1951, 1953–1958

In pure statistical terms, Juan Manuel Fangio is top of the pile. In seven seasons he became world champion five times and finished runner-up twice. He started all but three of his 51 Grand Prix on the front row and won 24 of them, giving him a win percentage of 47%, well clear of the next nearest driver. Fangio also won the Drivers' Championship with four different teams, another record that is likely to stand unchallenged. The first came with Alfa Romeo in 1951. The next came in 1954, a season that Fangio began with Maserati but switched to Mercedes part way through. It was the first of four consecutive championships. The next came behind the wheel of his Mercedes, in 1956 he drove a Ferrari, in 1957 he was back at Maserati. His success and ability to remain fast despite switching cars was the product of years spent learning his trade in his native Argentina. Fangio was able to control the heavy Italian-built monsters that dominated the first years of F1, using brute strength to turn the steering wheel as he slid through corners and relying on his great stamina to keep going in races that often lasted for more than three hours.

02 MICHAEL SCHUMACHER
1991–2006, 2010–2012

The first German world champion was as much a winning machine as the cars he drove. Michael Schumacher was supremely fit and able to make split-second decisions for lap after lap, driving his cars consistently on the limit of grip before returning to give his mechanics a detailed report. He finished in the top three in more than half the races he started; the proportion of podium finishes would have been even higher had he not returned for a largely unsuccessful three-year stint with Mercedes after his first retirement. Schumacher won two Drivers' Championships with Benetton in 1994 and 1995 before adding five on the trot with Ferrari from 2000 to 2004. At times he was unstoppable. He finished on the podium in all 17 races of the 2002 season, in 2004 he won 13 of 18 races to take the championship by a colossal margin. There were moments of controversy, too – a two-race ban in 1994 for ignoring a black flag, a crash with Hill in the last race of the same season and a similar collision with Villeneuve in 1997 that saw Schumacher stripped of all the points he had earned during the season – but nobody becomes a seven-time world champion without possessing a steely determination to win.

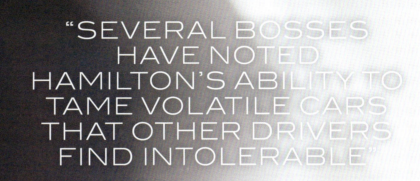

"SEVERAL BOSSES HAVE NOTED HAMILTON'S ABILITY TO TAME VOLATILE CARS THAT OTHER DRIVERS FIND INTOLERABLE"

01 LEWIS HAMILTON
2007–PRESENT

Nobody seriously expected any driver to come close to Schumacher's seven Drivers' Championship titles when he retired for a second time in 2012, so it was a surprise when one person managed it within seven years. Not only that, but it was Schumacher's replacement at Mercedes who matched his achievement. Hamilton was already a world champion when he joined the German team, having won the title with McLaren in 2008. He had graduated from the McLaren young driver programme and made an immediate impression in 2007, missing out on top spot to Räikkönen by a single point in the most impressive rookie season F1 has seen. He quickly gained a reputation as an all-round talent, setting quick times on various types of tracks and in different weather conditions. Hamilton is consistent, too. Several bosses have noted his ability to tame volatile cars that other drivers find intolerable. Hamilton added six more championship crowns with Mercedes, setting records for the most wins, podiums and pole positions by an F1 driver on the way, taking advantage of his team's dominance when the use of turbo-hybrid engines was allowed from 2014. And he isn't done yet. As the words on his helmet proclaim, 'Still I Rise.'

TOP 10
FORMULA ONE
RACES
OF ALL TIME

With over 1,000 races held across 34 countries, selecting the top ten greatest Grand Prix of all time is no easy feat...

N ot only is picking the greatest races endlessly subjective, but even the concept is contentious; what makes a race great? Is it the most dramatic, the most unpredictable, the strangest, the most beloved, the most surprising or the most intense?

In the end, it seems only right to include racing gems that embody as many of these traits as possible. Those overflowing with unexpected twists and turns, thrills and spills, outcomes and exchanges that live on in memory, while 'textbook' races fade away. The ones with dramatic highs and crushing lows. Perhaps those that fell victim to the elements; creating nail-biting near misses, spectacular crashes, daring overtakes, flurries of pit stops and penalties, pack reshuffles, and red flag restarts. The 'legendary' races that F1 fans bring up time and time again. The ones that go down in history as a racer's drive of his life, and of course those all-important championship deciders. What's more, with recent seasons fresher in the mind, it's easy to be swayed by races that happened in the last decade, while a favoured team, driver, circuit or season could also sway the line up.

Ultimately, not everyone will agree on the greatest top ten, but isn't that what makes Formula 1 so great? The suspense, the surprise and, of course, the controversy...

10 MORE TWIST AND TURNS THAN THE HUNGARORING ITSELF!

2014, HUNGARIAN GP, HUNGARORING

An unseasonable thunderstorm followed by a quickly drying track saw crashes, safety cars, a never-ending tide of tyre changes and several shuffles of the pack. Nico Rosberg led comfortably from the off, while teammate and championship rival, Lewis Hamilton, started from the pitlane after a disastrous qualifier in which his Mercedes caught fire. Daniel Ricciardo, either having a lucky day or timing his pit stops under the safety cars to perfection, was able to take and retake the lead. As the final laps closed in, Ricciardo launched a late charge, soaring past both Hamilton (who had climbed from last to second, infamously refusing team orders to let Rosberg pass), and leader Fernando Alonso whose 30-lap worn-out tyres held them both back, to take the chequered flag.

09 THREE-WAY TITLE RIVALRY EXPLODES DOWN UNDER
1986, AUSTRALIAN GP, ADELAIDE STREET CIRCUIT

The 1986 Grand Prix title was decided in Australia on the last race of the season; pitting bitter rivals Nigel Mansell, Alain Prost and Nelson Piquet against one another.

Polesitter Mansell had a lacklustre start that saw him drop to fourth by the end of the first lap, with his Brazilian teammate, Piquet, now out front. Keke Rosberg, in this, his Formula 1 swansong, took the lead a few laps later, holding the position until a puncture forced his retirement on lap 63. With Rosberg out, Mansell was promoted to third, which was enough to secure the title. However, disaster struck one lap later, and a blowout saw the Brit's hopes in tatters.

Keen to avoid a similar situation with Piquet, Williams called him in for fresh wheels, which left him 15 seconds behind the new leader – Prost. Despite an admirable late charge, closing the gap to just over four seconds, it wasn't enough to deny the Frenchman his second of four championships.

08 AND THEN THERE WERE THREE
1996, MONACO GP, MONACO STREET CIRCUIT

Dramatically foreshadowing what was to come, the race's wet and wild warm-up saw a succession of skids, near misses and even took Andrea Montermini out of the running.

Once the race started, a catalogue of mishaps whittled the 21 cars that started down to 13 by lap five, and seven by lap 68, with reasons for retirement including: accidents (six), mechanical problems (four), and collisions (four). A collision on the 68th circuit, caused by a spun-off Eddie Irvine trying to rejoin the race, created a three-way pile up with Mika Salo and Mika Häkkinen. By the end of the race only four drivers remained.

Olivier Panis took his first and only F1 victory, masterfully avoiding the carnage around him, while David Coulthard scooped second and Johnny Herbert third. Heinz-Harald Frentzen retired in the pits on the final lap, but was classified fourth.

07 THE 'WORST START' EVER
1998, BELGIAN GP, SPA-FRANCORCHAMPS

Living up to its reputation as the wettest circuit on the F1 calendar, the 1998 outing at Spa certainly delivered spills and thrills. The first of many came right out of the gate, as David Coulthard ploughed into the wall on turn one, taking out 13 cars with him, sending wheels and other mechanical debris flying through the smoke-shrouded air in a scene commentator Murray Walker described as the worst start he'd ever seen. A red flag restart saw the majority of drivers (those with spare cars) return to the track, but polesitter and current championship leader, Mika Häkkinen, collided almost instantly with Johnny Herbert. After snapping at race leader Damon Hill's tail, Michael Schumacher, who was in contention for the title against the now-retired Häkkinen, pushed in front on lap seven, building a 30-second lead until lap 24, when, attempting to lap his then good friend Coulthard, slammed into the back of his McLaren after the Scot, who was blinded by spray, had slowed on the racing line. Despite attempting to continue with three wheels, the German was forced to retire and in a moment of unforgettable F1 history, stormed into the McLaren garage to confront Coulthard. Elsewhere, Giancarlo Fisichella's Benetton burst into flames after colliding with Shinji Nakano, and with just a handful of cars left, Hill took the chequered flag.

06 LEWIS HAMILTON'S SOLO RESTART
2021, HUNGARIAN GP, HUNGARORING

Despite a Mercedes front row lockout, only Lewis Hamilton got away cleanly. Valtteri Bottas shunted the back of Lando Norris, who together slipped across the wet bend, taking out the two Red Bulls. Meanwhile Lance Stroll collided with Charles Leclerc, which forced Daniel Ricciardo to spin. The Australian and Max Verstappen continued, but the race was red-flagged soon after. All but Hamilton chose to dive into the pits (where Kimi Räikkönen accidentally took out Nikita Mazepin) to swap to slicks, leading to one of the most bizarre sights in motorsport history; a lonely Hamilton waiting on an empty grid for lights out. By lap five it was Frenchman Esteban Ocon in the lead as George Russell, who emerged first from the pitlane after illegally queue jumping, was penalised and Hamilton, realising his tyre error, boxed. At one point both Alpines were ahead, with Fernando Alonso first, until he boxed and returned to fourth. It was here the Spaniard masterfully held back the pack for the majority of the race, allowing his French teammate to pull away, with only Sebastian Vettel and Carlos Sainz behind him. Hamilton's chance to overtake came on lap 65 when Alonso's Alpine locked up, then with only three laps remaining took Sainz, but there wasn't enough time to catch Ocon who claimed his and Alpine's first victory. Hamilton was awarded second (Vettel being disqualified for lacking enough fuel to sample), and Sainz third.

05 THE LAST-MINUTE SWITCHEROO
1964, MEXICAN GP, MAGDALENA MIXHUCA CIRCUIT

The last race of the 1964 season set the stage for a three-way championship showdown between John Surtees, Graham Hill and Jim Clark. Leading from the off, Clark left his two rivals in his dust, with Hill taking on Surtees' Ferrari teammate Lorenzo Bandini for third, while Surtees dropped to fifth. Later Bandini and Hill clashed, sending the Brit's BRM spinning into the barrier. With Surtees also seemingly dropping off the radar, it looked as though Clark would edge the title. However, with less than a lap to go, Clark suffered an oil leak and his Lotus seized, temporarily handing Hill the title. But Ferrari realised if Surtees moved up one place to second (held by its other driver, Bandini) he'd be champion. The problem was there was only one place on the track to convey the message, but the team's desperate signals were spotted and understood. The last-minute switch was made just before the finish, allowing Surtees to grab the title by one point.

04 SENNA VERSUS PROST
1988, JAPANESE GP, SUZUKA CIRCUIT

The Alain Prost/Ayrton Senna rivalry was one of the most fierce and polarising the sport has ever known, hitting its peak during their period as teammates at McLaren in 1988 and 1989, and continuing when Prost fled to Ferrari in 1990. All three of these consecutive championships were settled on the penultimate race of the season: Japan, and arguably could all feature here with their many twists, turns and controversy, but it's the first of these championship deciders, which is known as one of the Brazilian's greatest ever drives, that makes the top ten.

After stalling on pole, Senna used the circuit's sloping grid to try to bump start his car. Although successful, many immediately wrote off his title shot, as his McLaren crawled out of the starting gate and he dropped to 14th. However, it quickly picked up speed and driving like a man possessed, Senna stormed through the herd, passing seven on his first lap, and making it to second by lap 20. With leader Prost stuck behind backmarkers on lap 27, Senna slipstreamed on the inside line, and held the lead through to the finish, clinching the title for the first time.

03 BUTTON'S BRILLIANCE AT THE LAST
2011, CANADIAN GP, CIRCUIT GILLES VILLENEUVE

Coming into the race with an incredible 58-point lead over Lewis Hamilton in second, Sebastian Vettel looked set to take the title. But as with every race where heavy rain is involved, assumption goes out of the window.

Racing got underway on lap five (released from the safety car) and it wasn't long before the pack was stirred. First to clash were Hamilton and Mark Webber, but it was his brush with his McLaren teammate that would send Hamilton out of the running. Mid-race, Jenson Button served a drive-through penalty for speeding under the safety car, returning to the field 15th. Torrential rain paused the drama for over two hours (making it the longest GP in history) but after a red flag restart, Button was at it again, this time colliding with Fernando Alonso. With DRS enabled, Button zoomed past car after car. After the sixth safety car, the Brit took Webber and Michael Schumacher in the same lap, moving into second, then a late turn by leader Vettel was all Button needed to win.

02 A LAST CORNER TITLE CLINCHER
2008, BRAZILIAN GP, INTERLAGOS

Two challengers stood to gain the title coming into the 2008 finale – Felipe Massa, who'd had his best ever season, was welcomed by his home crowd hoping for their first champion since Ayrton Senna (1991), and Lewis Hamilton, coming off the back of his rookie season where he narrowly missed out on the championship to Kimi Räikkönen, after warring with Fernando Alonso. This time, however, with a five-point advantage, the Brit only needed to finish fifth to be champion.

A sudden downpour delayed the start with teams quickly switching tyres, but things looked promising for the Brazilian with the Ferrari on pole and Hamilton down in fourth. An early crash saw David Coulthard end his F1 career on the side of the track, which was by now quickly drying and provoking another flurry of tyre changes. This is when Hamilton dropped to seventh, presumably taking himself out of the title race. But quick to display his now trademark grit, Hamilton clawed his way back to fifth; as it stood, enough to win the title.

Light rain saw new tyres for all the racers, except the Toyotas, one of which was Timo Glock. Robert Kubica unlapped himself, passing Hamilton and slowing the Brit's pace, while a momentary slip-up saw him run wide, allowing Sebastian Vettel to sneak past and steal that all-important fifth place, just as Massa cruised across the finish line.

Emotionally overjoyed and overwhelmed, the Brazilian's fans, friends, family and Ferrari team exploded into euphoric celebration. However the race wasn't quite complete. Yet to finish, Glock struggled for grip as his inappropriate tyres were failing him in the rain, and were no match for Hamilton, who skilfully passed him on the last corner, grabbing the title by a single point and silencing the now shell-shocked crowd.

01 CHAMPIONSHIP DECIDER IN SHUFFLING SPECTACULAR
2012, BRAZILIAN GP, INTERLAGOS

Featuring a record-breaking (until 2016) 147 successful overtakes, the 2012 championship decider went down in F1 history as one of the most thrilling, where the pack, the leader, and the title winner, changed at breakneck speed throughout the increasingly wet 71 laps.

Heading into the last race on the calendar, the championship was Sebastian Vettel's for the taking but there was a chance that if Fernando Alonso placed high enough, the Spaniard would be crowned the victor.

Vettel had high hopes, starting in fourth but an early tangle with Bruno Senna left him facing the wrong way and sporting damaged side pods, dropping him to last. Now with the championship blown wide open, Alonso powered through from eighth to third. Meanwhile Nico Hülkenberg took the lead (for the first time in his F1 career), but the decision to stay out on slicks cost him when a spin handed Lewis Hamilton the front spot. Later the two collided, taking the latter out of his final race for McLaren, and seeing Jenson Button creep up into first.

Light drizzle evolved into heavy rain, and although Vettel was one of the first to pit, a broken radio system meant his team were left unprepared for his arrival, resulting in a painfully longer than usual pit stop. Ferrari, however, used their well-timed break to swap driver positions, allowing Alonso to take Felipe Massa's second.

Vettel fought on, but with conditions becoming increasingly treacherous a crash seemed inevitable, and sure enough Paul di Resta's accident on lap 70 meant the season would finish behind a safety car. Bad news for second-place Alonso who although protected by his Ferrari teammate to his rear, had no choice but to trundle along in the spray of Button's McLaren, who crossed the finishing line first (for the last time in his career).

The safety car was welcomed by Vettel, however, who would safely finish in sixth, enough to beat his rival by three points and see him become the youngest triple champion since Michael Schumacher (whose last race this would become). The young German called it his toughest race, claiming in an interview that "everything that could go wrong went wrong. I think you guys had your show and we had to really fight right until the end."

TOP 10
FORMULA ONE
TEAMS
OF ALL TIME

A rundown of the ten best car marques ever in Formula 1, and why we have chosen them

Any list of 'top teams' in Formula 1 that is determined solely by points accrued is going to favour more modern teams, as there are more races each year, and more points available to more cars. And while longevity is a factor, how much weight should it be given? How do you rate Brawn, for example, who competed for just a single season, winning eight of 17 races, with their drivers finishing first and third in the championship?

This top ten takes into account a myriad of factors in assessing the greatest teams, though inevitably the cold hard stats of wins, poles and points are difficult to ignore completely. Teams such as BRM and Tyrrell were unlucky to just miss out on the list, while others such as Force India and Sauber, though accruing a lot of points overall, just don't have the race wins or podium finishes to make a stronger case for inclusion. Attempting to rank this top ten was a task even more fraught with possibilities, but hopefully you'll find plenty to agree – and disagree – with over the choices that were ultimately made.

Fernando Alonso drives the 2005 world championship-winning Renault around the circuit in Jerez, Spain

10 RENAULT
CONSTRUCTORS' TITLES: 2 | RACE WINS: 35

With 400 race starts, Renault have bagged 103 podiums and two World Drivers' titles in the same years as they claimed the Constructors' titles (2005 and 2006), both by Fernando Alonso. Points-wise they rank as high as sixth in the all-time standings, but they drop a handful of places in our table because they claimed significantly more poles (51) than wins. Rebranded as Alpine for the 2021 season, they took their first race win through Esteban Ocon in Hungary.

09 BENETTON
CONSTRUCTORS' TITLES: 1 | RACE WINS: 27

Once upon a time, Benetton were best known for their clothing range, but they also had a successful period in F1 in the mid-1990s, although the French team were based in the UK throughout. The F1 team only won the Constructors' title once, in 1995, but also won two Drivers' titles (1994 and 1995), courtesy of Michael Schumacher. The German ace accounted for 19 of Benetton's 27 race wins. The team have an outstanding conversion rate from only 15 pole positions, with 102 podiums and 861.5 points from 260 starts – all impressive figures. The 2001 season was their final one; subsequent to that they rebranded as Renault.

Johnny Herbert scored his maiden victory at the British Grand Prix at Silverstone with Benetton in 1995

Juan Manuel Fangio wins the 1951 French Grand Prix in an Alfa Romeo

08 ALFA ROMEO
CONSTRUCTORS' TITLES: 0 | RACE WINS: 10

A very famous name in motorsports, Alfa Romeo have competed in F1 on several occasions and returned to the sport in 2019 (having not taken part since the 1985 season), when Sauber were rebranded as Alfa Romeo Racing. By far their most successful period was the two years from 1950 to 1951 when first Giuseppe Farina and then Juan Manuel Fangio won consecutive World Drivers' titles. Alfa Romeo would have taken the Constructors' title in both years, if that competition had been in existence then. Indeed, the famous 158 model won every race in 1950 and its evolution, the 159, won four out of the seven official races the following year. Sadly, Alfa Romeo have never been competitive since those days.

07 COOPER CAR COMPANY
CONSTRUCTORS' TITLES: 2 | RACE WINS: 16

That the Cooper-Climax T51 was a revolutionary design was more by accident than design. Father and son Charles and John Cooper moved the engine to the back of their car to make engineering access easier, not because they thought it would have benefits in terms of weight distribution or handling. In the event, it had both and the T51 – in the hands of Jack Brabham – won both the Drivers' and Constructors' Championships in 1959 and 1960. The 1959 Drivers' Championship went down to the wire, but the Constructors' title was more comfortable, with Cooper winning five of the eight races (and three of the five non-championship races). In 1960, Brabham reeled off five consecutive Grand Prix victories to comfortably retain his Drivers' title and with Bruce McLaren adding a sixth win (out of nine races), Cooper won their second Constructors' title in a row. In total points won, the Cooper-Climax stands only 16th in the all-time table, but its influence was felt way beyond that, and the impact it had on car design cannot be overstated.

Stirling Moss drives the Cooper-Climax T51 at the 1960 Dutch Grand Prix

06 LOTUS
CONSTRUCTORS' TITLES: 7 | RACE WINS: 79

The Lotus 25 designed by Colin Chapman in 1962 was a truly revolutionary car. With it, Chapman completely disregarded previously accepted norms, such as a spaceframe construction method, and replaced them with a 'bathtub' structure in which aluminium panels were formed around a series of internal bulkheads. This ushered in the era of full monocoque construction and a semi-reclined driving position. Fuel tanks were located to the side of the 'tub'. It resulted in the best handling car of its time. There was a payoff, however. The Lotus 25 was fast but fragile and a large number of drivers were killed or seriously injured driving it. In 1967, Lotus became the

The great Jim Clark drives the iconic Lotus 25 to victory at the 1963 Dutch Grand Prix

first team to introduce aerofoil wings, which were initially bolted directly to the suspension and were supported by slender struts. The chassis configuration was further refined and the engine was bolted to the monocoque at one end and to the suspension and gearbox at the other. Virtually all F1 cars have been built this way ever since. In addition to the team's seven Constructors' titles, Lotus cars have been driven to six Drivers' titles, for Jim Clark (two), Graham Hill, Jochen Rindt, Emerson Fittipaldi and Mario Andretti.

05 WILLIAMS
CONSTRUCTORS' TITLES: 9 | RACE WINS: 114

Nigel Mansell is the driver most often associated with Williams' success, possibly because the 1992 FW14B model was so far ahead of its time that it utterly dominated the championship that year. The brilliant Adrian Newey made the most of the new computer-controlled suspension, enabling the car to run at a much lower ride height than previously possible, which led to spectacular aerodynamic gains. In 16 races Mansell won nine times; he was also on pole 14 times and posted the fastest lap on eight occasions. In fact, the FW14B was a modification (albeit a startling one) of the 1979 FW07, which won consecutive Constructors' titles in 1980 and 1981 and Alan Jones the 1980 Drivers' title. The FW07 was based largely on the Lotus, which preceded it as the car to beat, but improved it by moving the cockpit and sidepods – and therefore the centre of aerodynamic pressure – further forward. Keke Rosberg (1982), Nelson Piquet (1987), Alain Prost (1993), Damon Hill (1996) and Jacques Villeneuve (1997) have also won Drivers' titles with Williams. Williams have posted 133 fastest laps, 128 poles and a points total of 3,584 to date, making them worthy recipients of a top-five placing in this table.

» Sparks fly, appropriately, as the Williams FW14B was in total control of the 1992 championship

World champion Sebastian Vettel crosses the finish line to win the 2013 Malaysian Grand Prix

04 RED BULL
CONSTRUCTORS' TITLES: 5 | RACE WINS:92

Red Bull Racing have quickly established themselves as a force to be reckoned with. Another to benefit from the genius of Newey, who they snatched from McLaren in 2005, Red Bull Racing took a few years to find the chassis and the engines they wanted but by 2010, were the dominant force in F1. That year the Drivers' title was hotly contested, with Red Bull drivers Sebastian Vettel and Mark Webber finishing first and third respectively, with Vettel only snatching the title from Alonso by virtue of winning the last two Grand Prix. But with nine race wins from the 19 rounds, Red Bull enjoyed a comfortable margin of victory over McLaren. Red Bull and Vettel proceeded to win the Constructors' and Drivers' titles for the next three seasons. The 2013 season saw Vettel win the last nine races of the season, a staggering feat and one which brought him the title by a margin of 155 points. That mark was almost beaten by Max Verstappen, who took the title by 146 points from Charles Leclerc in 2022. Red Bull notched up 596 points compared to the 360 of their closest rivals (Mercedes). Ninety-two victories from 325 starts represents a winning percentage of 26.5%; poles (81) and fastest laps (84) are roughly in line with victories, while 234 podiums equates to a high level of consistency.

03 MCLAREN
CONSTRUCTORS' TITLES: 8 | RACE WINS: 183

At 20%, McLaren's percentage of wins (183) to starts (924) is slightly lower than that of Red Bull, but they have the edge because of their longevity in the sport. McLaren first competed in F1 in 1966, at the Monaco Grand Prix, making them the second-oldest F1 team after Ferrari. It was an inauspicious start as Bruce McLaren retired after just nine laps because of an oil leak. There followed many seasons of mediocrity, but the tide started turning when the team merged with Ron Dennis's Project Four Formula 2 team in 1980, which shared a sponsor in (cigarette manufacturer) Philip Morris. That merger brought in not just the brilliance of Dennis, but his designer John Barnard, who was the instigator of a carbonfibre chassis to replace the aluminium alloy ones. Barnard also introduced the 'coke bottle' effect: this teardrop-shaped profile speeds up airflow to the rear wing and reduces drag, for maximum aerodynamic efficiency. Constructors' titles followed in 1984, 1985, 1988, 1989, 1990 and 1991, while Drivers' titles were also won in each of those years, plus 1986. Of course, it didn't hurt having drivers of the quality of Niki Lauda, Alain Prost and Ayrton Senna, but the cars would have been competitive whoever was driving them.

 Niki Lauda drives a McLaren to victory at the 1984 British Grand Prix at Brands Hatch

02 MERCEDES
CONSTRUCTORS' TITLES: 8 | RACE WINS: 125

It would be easy to say that Mercedes' place as a top team owes everything to Lewis Hamilton, whose record-equalling seven consecutive Drivers' titles have brought the same number of Constructors' titles to the marque. Juan Manuel Fangio had won Drivers' titles in 1954 and 1955, but as he drove both Mercedes and Maseratis in those years, it's hard to say they were definitively Mercedes triumphs. Under the solo Mercedes banner, the marque has won an incredible 125 out of 271 races; 103 of those wins by Hamilton. And yet the team were not really a new one in 2010; they were born out of the 2009 Brawn team that had won both the Drivers' and Constructors' titles that year. Furthermore, Ross Brawn himself stayed on for a further three years after the takeover, and Mercedes benefitted from his wealth of knowledge. Nevertheless, Hamilton is statistically the greatest F1 driver of all time, and his undoubted skill – and close involvement in the development of the car – is what has brought Mercedes 136 poles, 281 podiums and 100 fastest laps. Not to mention almost 7,000 points, the second-highest total overall and the highest points-per-race ratio.

 Lewis Hamilton steers the impressive Mercedes car round the circuit during practice for the Bahrain Grand Prix in 2020

01 FERRARI
CONSTRUCTORS' TITLES: 16 | RACE WINS: 242

Ferrari are the most evocative name in Formula 1. By most metrics they are also the most successful. Ferrari cars have won 16 Constructors' titles and 15 Drivers' titles. In the same way that Mercedes have benefitted from the skill of Lewis Hamilton, Ferrari's records owe much to the five consecutive titles by Michael Schumacher. But other greats such as Alberto Ascari, Mike Hawthorn, John Surtees, Kimi Räikkönen and, of course, Lauda have also become world champions in a Ferrari and the marque has never been content to rest on its laurels. The John Barnard-inspired 639/640 Ferrari was a masterpiece of design. It introduced the concept of paddle-operated semi-automatic transmission, with the deletion of a gear lever facilitating a narrower cockpit for a lower frontal area. The gear changes were quicker than any driver could manage, meaning he could keep both hands on the wheel, and certain corners could be entered at greater speeds, which cut lap times.

The F2004 model was a further quantum leap forward – its shortened wheelbase brought the weight distribution forward and relieved some of the load on the overworked rear tyres. The rear suspension was mounted directly onto the engine,

Schumacher and Ferrari were a force to be reckoned with during the 1990s and 2000s

and it had a tiny gearbox (weighing under 10kg). It was a beautiful car in which Schumacher won 13 out of 18 races in the 2004 season. With Rubens Barrichello winning twice, it meant that Ferrari were only defeated on three occasions in the whole year. Schumacher finished on 148 points, Barrichello on 114 and Jenson Button on 85. In the Constructors' Championship Ferrari scored 262 points, with BAR-Honda in second on less than half, 119.

But their success is more wide-ranging than just the odd dominant season. Ferrari hold numerous records in F1: they are the oldest team still competing, the only team which uses their own engines and chassis, their cars have started in 1,051 races and won 242 (one of the best win-to-races ratio and over a longer period than their rivals). They have posted 242 pole positions and 258 fastest laps, all in those iconic cars with their red livery and, of course, the Prancing Horse logo. If there is currently a hiatus in their championship-winning days (their last Constructors' title was in 2008), history tells us that it will not last.

TOP 10

FORMULA ONE
TRACKS
OF ALL TIME

Which are F1's most iconic circuits, and why? What combination of factors makes them memorable? Find out with this Top 10 guide...

t's impossible to put together an objective list of the 'best' Formula 1 circuits. Is it the circuit that the drivers like the most? Or the ones which afford the best fan experience? How about the ones that have provided the closest finishes, the most memorable moments (good or bad)?

Then there are the ones that have the most history, take place in the most incredible surroundings or the ones which push the envelope that little bit further in terms of technology. Some circuits might provide the perfect visceral experience to those who attend in person, while others might best be viewed at a distance in order to take in their full splendour. Clearly all these factors – and many more besides – can influence opinion. How much weight you afford any one criterion over any other will depend on personal preferences. One aspect which is much improved from yesteryear is safety (Frenchman Jules Bianchi is the only driver to die as a result of an F1 crash since 1994, and that was a freak accident rather than a failure of safety measures on the circuit), and for that we should all be grateful. Here then is our totally subjective and very personal take on our favourite circuits from around the world.

10 CIRCUIT OF THE AMERICAS
USA

COTA, as it's colloquially known, is a new circuit, opened in 2012. It is the first circuit in the United States to be purpose-built for F1 (though other forms of motor racing also now take part on it) and the involvement of legendary F1 architect Hermann Tilke ensures its suitability. COTA is a 5.5km (3.4mi) track that incorporates ideas from several well-established European F1 circuits. Reaction to it from the drivers has mostly been positive, and it looks set to become an established feature of the F1 calendar.

The purpose-built COTA circuit in Austin, Texas

09 MARINA BAY
SINGAPORE

A street circuit designed by Hermann Tilke then modified by KBR, Inc, the Marina Bay Street Circuit is situated in downtown Singapore at a harbourside location similar to Monaco. The track is just over 5km (3mi) long. On its debut in 2008, the drivers criticised its excessive bumpiness. Constant, if small, modifications have taken place every year since, but it still boasts the dubious record of the only circuit to feature at least one appearance of the safety car in every race to date. It owes its place here to the astonishing spectacle of a night race (practice and qualifying sessions also take place at night) and all the added drama that brings.

The Marina Bay street circuit in Singapore hosts a spectacular night race

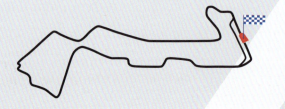

08 NÜRBURGRING
GERMANY

Not so long ago, Germany hosted two races in the F1 calendar – the German Grand Prix usually took place at Hockenheim, while the race at the Nürburgring was known as the European Grand Prix. Originally a huge 28km (17mi) circuit which stretched up into the forests, it was widely regarded as a very dangerous track on account of its lack of safety barriers and being too big to marshall properly. Five drivers lost their lives there. It was also the scene of Niki Lauda's infamous accident in 1976, which he was lucky to survive, and which led to the construction of a new shorter, safer course. The bigger beast, once dubbed 'The Green Hell' by Jackie Stewart, lies slumbering next to it.

The Nürburgring in Germany – beautiful but treacherous

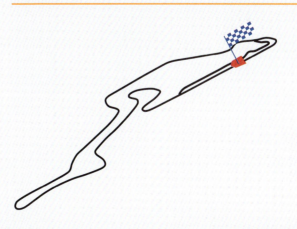

07 INTERLAGOS
BRAZIL

F1's most famous counterclockwise circuit, Interlagos is Brazil's primary racetrack and first hosted the Brazilian Grand Prix in 1973. Officially called the Autódromo José Carlos Pace, it has become widely known as Interlagos (meaning 'between two lakes') because it is situated in between two constructed lakes built to supply São Paulo with water and electric power. It owes its status to being situated on naturally hilly ground, with its many inclines demanding of both cars and drivers, and also its counterclockwise layout, which means the centrifugal forces exert the opposite impact on the drivers from what they are used to.

Extensively remodelled from 1990, it is now a shorter 4.3km (2.7mi) track and it has also been completely relaid to address earlier problems with the bumpiness of the surface. An astonishingly fast track with opportunities for dramatic overtaking, Interlagos benefits from passionate local fans who have witnessed Brazilian drivers Emerson Fittipaldi, Nelson Piquet, Ayrton Senna, Felipe Massa and Pace (after whom the circuit is named) win there, though they suffered heartbreak when Hamilton snatched the world title from Massa on the last lap in 2008.

 The Interlagos circuit is located in São Paulo

06 ÖSTERREICHRING
AUSTRIA

The original Österreichring circuit was a very fast track where almost every corner was long and high-speed. Built in the scenic Styrian mountains, it was also full of trees and while drivers enjoyed the speeds they could race it, there were also concerns that it was dangerous. With cars in the late 1980s becoming too fast for the track (Piquet took pole in 1987 at a speed of 159mph/256km/h), the cramped starting grid and narrow pit lanes were deemed unsafe and the venue was abandoned for ten years. In 1997, though, the layout was shortened to 4.3km (2.7mi) and redesigned by Tilke to remove many of the long, sweeping curves. Known as the A1-Ring it again hosted F1 from 1997-2003. Another hiatus followed before the circuit, now the Red Bull Ring, reopened to F1 in 2014. In each of the 2020 and 2021 seasons the circuit hosted two F1 races (as a result of other countries dropping out because of the pandemic); in 2021 Max Verstappen won both from pole for two of his ten race victories in claiming his first world championship title.

The Red Bull Ring, opened in 2014, is safer but just as spectacular as its predecessor, the Österreichring

05 MONACO
MONACO

The most famous street circuit in the world, nestled amid extreme wealth, sees an influx of celebrities to watch the show every year. The setting is stunning – it is virtually impossible to take a bad photo at the Monaco Grand Prix, with its winding streets and Mediterranean backdrop. It isn't just a motor race, it's an event. A week-long jamboree that attracts the great and the good to play and to party. The track itself is a narrow one of 3.3km (just over 2mi) with frequent elevation changes and, of course, tight corners as it weaves around the harbour. It also has a tunnel, which adds an extra element of skill as drivers emerge from the gloom onto the fastest portion of the track. Interestingly, if the circuit wasn't already on the calendar it would be prohibited from joining the roster on safety grounds. The Monaco Grand Prix is part of the Triple Crown of Motorsport (the other events being the Indy 500 and the Le Mans 24-Hour Race); Graham Hill is the only driver in history to have won all three. Only the difficulty in overtaking, which occasionally leads to a processional race, prevents Monaco from being higher up in our ranking.

The Nouvelle chicane takes drivers around the harbour at the Monaco Grand Prix

04 SILVERSTONE
ENGLAND

The location of Silverstone, on the Northamptonshire-Buckinghamshire border on a disused RAF airfield, is hardly a glamorous setting. And yet, the grand old lady of F1 circuits retains a certain allure thanks to the presence of knowledgeable (but not blinkered) fans and its history as the oldest race in the F1 World Championship calendar. In spite of changes over the years, both major and minor, the essence of Silverstone has always been its fast, challenging corners that demand the full attention of the drivers, and a steady rhythm to manoeuvre round them. In its current guise the track is 5.9km (3.7mi). Remodelling in 1990 turned it into a more technical track, and further changes in 1995 saw improvements to the run-off area at the legendary Stowe Corner; this was at a time when many Grand Prix circuits were modified in the wake of the deaths of Senna and Roland Ratzenberger at Imola the previous year. More developments came in 2010 with the new 'Arena' configuration being used and the following year a new pit complex was constructed between Club and Abbey Corners, with the start/finish line also being moved there. Lewis Hamilton has won eight times at Silverstone, three more than any other driver.

The new pit lane complex and start/finish straight at Silverstone

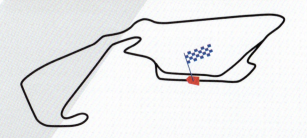

03 MONZA
ITALY

Monza has a somewhat chequered history in terms of its safety record. In 1928, Emilio Materassi went off the track and into the unprotected grandstand opposite the pits, killing himself and 27 spectators, and injuring a further 26. This is the worst accident in F1 history. Five years later, the 1933 race saw three drivers killed, two in the heats and another in the race itself. Further fatalities occurred in 1961 – when German count Wolfgang von Trips suffered an airborne crash that killed him and 15 spectators – and, most infamously, in 1970 with the death of Jochen Rindt. Rindt was killed during practice but was so dominant in the championship up to that point, no other driver was able to subsequently overhaul his points total so he became posthumous world champion. The great Swedish driver Ronnie Peterson also died as a result of injuries sustained in a 1978 crash at Monza. It would be unfair to say Monza was famous only for negative stories, though.

The track, which today is 5.8km (3.6mi) long, has always been fast and spectacular, with high-speed cornering and the ability to slipstream off other cars of paramount importance. Coupled with the passionate fans, Monza continues to retain an ambience of unique theatricality.

High-speed corners – and the chaos that can ensue – have always been a feature at Monza

02 SUZUKA
JAPAN

The unusual setting of being next to – and partly within – a funfair, make a Grand Prix at Suzuka a special event. Designed by John Hugenholtz, the 5.8km (3.6mi) track is in a figure of eight, which maximises viewing opportunities for the fans. A highlight in Suzuka's history is the three consecutive battles between Prost and Senna between 1988 and 1990. After the Brazilian had pipped the Frenchman in 1988, the subsequent two years saw the driver leading the championship refuse to yield to his rival and instead instigate crashes, which led to both cars retiring. Since then Suzuka has often played host to a decisive battle in the destination of the world title. One tragic footnote is the accident suffered by Jules Bianchi in 2014. He crashed into a crane that was removing a damaged car; after nine months in a coma, Bianchi died of his injuries. From the off, though, drivers have loved the circuit, which is incredibly fast but technically difficult, particularly in the esses section, demanding high levels of skill to master.

The Suzuka circuit is a favourite of many drivers, particularly its challenging esses section

» Early morning over the Eau Rouge at Spa-Francorchamps, one of the most demanding corners in Grand Prix racing

01 SPA-FRANCORCHAMPS
BELGIUM

The Spa-Francorchamps circuit has two distinct iterations: the one which originated in 1925 and lasted until 1970, and the one that has been in use since 1983. To take first things first, the old Spa was a 14km (8.7mi) circuit with ultra high-speed corners, making it one of the most challenging circuits in motorsport. It was brutal both physically and mentally and the unforgiving track was often accompanied by unpredictable weather with some sections drying out quicker than others. In 1960, two drivers were killed during the race while Mike Taylor and Stirling Moss both suffered bad crashes in practice – the former never raced again while the latter missed most of the rest of the season. From 1970 the Belgian Grand Prix alternated between two circuits, at Zolder and Nivelles-Baulers, while Spa was shortened to 7km (4.3mi) by cutting out the parts that had previously spun out into the countryside with all the attendant risks posed by telegraph poles, trees, embankments and stone walls.

Spa mark two was an immediate hit with drivers and fans. The circuit's signature section is known as Eau Rouge, though it's actually a two-part section where the bottom part is Eau Rouge (after the river which runs under it) and the top part is Le Raidillon, but it's always known collectively as Eau Rouge. The new circuit removed the kinks from this challenging section but you still had to change direction right at the point where the circuit shifted from downhill to uphill. And then there's Pouhon, which Lewis Hamilton once described as his favourite left-hand corner in the world: "It's swooping and downhill so you arrive there at incredible speeds. Not much room for error." Which sums up the whole Spa experience. A circuit that demands total commitment to hustling a car through ultra-fast corners with minimum adhesion. Damon Hill says its turns are the sort where "you find out about yourself as a racing driver." And Spa is often won by a great driver – Michael Schumacher holds the record with six wins. Ultimately, Spa allows drivers to race fast. Overtaking opportunities are plentiful, and the uncertain weather heightens the skill levels required. What more could anyone ask for in an F1 circuit?

TOP 10
FORMULA ONE
BOSSES
OF ALL TIME

The drivers may capture the public's imagination, but the most important figure for the teams is the team principal. Here we salute ten of the best

Formula 1 team principals are the figureheads of their teams. They arrived in that exalted position by a variety of routes – many are, or were, drivers themselves. Some fashioned teams in their own image and were synonymous with that team, like Colin Chapman, Ken Tyrrell and Sir Frank Williams. Others moved between teams, lending their expertise to a number of different roles.

Some won hatfuls of world titles, while others had to be content with one or two, but all have to be experts in dealing with a myriad of interests, often competing ones. Not only do they have to keep two drivers more or less equally happy (even when those drivers are primarily competing against each other), but they have to manage the team of engineers and technical wizards, deal with the press and public demands, step up when things go wrong and watch drivers take the glory when things go right. It requires a tricky and rare mix of abilities, which is why the best ones have become almost as widely known as the drivers themselves. Here are ten of the very best.

10 TOM WALKINSHAW
BENETTON (1991–1994), LIGIER (1995–1996), FOOTWORK (1996), ARROWS (1997–2002)

The only man to feature on our list who hasn't won a world title as a team principal, Tom Walkinshaw nevertheless deserves a place because of his sterling work over 11 years for Benetton, Ligier, Footwork and Arrows. A moderately successful driver across various forms of motorsport, Walkinshaw hit the big time when he founded his own team, Tom Walkinshaw Racing (TWR), at the age of just 30. He had a hand in recruiting Michael Schumacher to Benetton and then-world champion Damon Hill to Arrows in 1997.

» TWR boss Tom Walkinshaw at the 1996 German Grand Prix at Hockenheim

09 FLAVIO BRIATORE
BENETTON (1990–1997, 2000–2001), RENAULT (2002–2009)

Flavio Briatore's name will forever be associated with the 'Crashgate' scandal of 2008 when he was accused of telling Nelson Piquet to crash deliberately to help teammate Fernando Alonso win the race. Briatore was banned for life but his ban was later overturned by a French tribunal. The flamboyant Italian was in charge when Benetton won the 1995 Constructors' title, and a decade later repeated the feat with Renault. He won a third title as team principal the following year, 2006. Briatore is an astute businessman with interests in nightclubs, restaurants, holiday resorts, politics and, of course, Queens Park Rangers football club. He has had relationships with supermodels Naomi Campbell, Heidi Klum and Elisabetta Gregoraci, and has had children with the latter two.

« Briatore celebrates at the 2006 Monaco Grand Prix

Tyrrell speaking with driver Jackie Stewart

08 KEN TYRRELL
MATRA (1968–1969), TYRRELL (1970–1998)

Ken Tyrrell (he was christened Robert Kenneth but always went by 'Ken'), famously used a woodshed as his first workshop. A flair for spotting talent resulted in him contracting Jackie Stewart for his Junior team (future F1 world champions Jody Scheckter and John Surtees were other drivers whose ability he recognised early on). Initially, Tyrell joined forces with French firm Matra and the team raced under the Matra banner, bringing Stewart his first Drivers' title and the team a Constructors' title. Rebranded as Tyrrell, the team won two further Drivers' titles for Stewart in 1971 and 1973. The former also saw Tyrrell win his second Constructors' title, this time under his own name. But in 1973 Lotus, with Emerson Fittipaldi and Ronnie Peterson driving, took the Constructors' title. Lotus had the faster car(s), but the Tyrrell's reliability meant Stewart retired only once, compared to four and six retirements respectively for Fittipaldi and Peterson. However, the death of second driver François Cevert during the 1973 season led to Stewart's retirement and the team gradually slipped out of contention.

Australian Jack Brabham won three world titles as a driver, his first two in a Cooper-Climax in 1959 and 1960. The third came in a car bearing his own name, making him the only driver ever to win the championship in a car of his own name. That came in 1966, and the following year teammate Denny Hulme won his only world title, also in a Brabham, giving Brabham two World Constructors' titles to go with his three Drivers' titles. After his retirement, the Brabham marque won two further titles in 1981 and 1983 (under the ownership of Bernie Ecclestone, with Nelson Piquet at the wheel). Brabham was later knighted for services to motorsport and the winner's trophy at the Australian Grand Prix is named after him.

Brabham in a Brabham-Ford BT26A at the Italian Grand Prix, Monza, 1969

06 JEAN TODT
FERRARI (1993–2007)

When Jean Todt took over as team principal at Ferrari in 1993, it had been ten years since F1's most famous team had won the Constructors' title. It took a further six seasons before they claimed it again, but in that time, Todt had built a truly formidable team. Not only had he signed Michael Schumacher as a driver, he had also brought in Rory Byrne and Ross Brawn, two of the greatest technical minds to have graced the sport. Todt was the first non-Italian to be team principal at the Scuderia, and as such brought a subtly different aesthetic to the team. Ferrari embarked on an impressive run of dominance in the sport, claiming six consecutive Constructors' titles (and five Drivers' titles) from 1999 to 2004. After two years of being pipped by Renault, they returned to winning ways in 2007 and 2008, taking two more Constructors' Championships, though the second of these came after Todt had ended his direct involvement with the day-to-day running of the team (he remained a member of the board). But seven Constructors' titles is still a pretty good haul.

« Todt focusing on the challenge ahead, as the practice session for the 1996 Portuguese Grand Prix is about to begin

05 TOTO WOLFF
MERCEDES (2013–PRESENT)

Torger 'Toto' Wolff is another example of a decent racing driver becoming an outstanding team principal. He had some success in the Austrian and German Formula Ford championships in the 1990s, but his achievements since taking over at Mercedes-McLaren have been exceptional. Wolff is in charge of every aspect of Mercedes-Benz's motorsport operations. From 2014 to 2020, Mercedes won seven consecutive Constructors' titles, beating the record held by Ferrari. They also won all seven Drivers' titles, courtesy of Lewis Hamilton. Although Hamilton was controversially beaten to the Drivers' title in 2021, Mercedes retained the Constructors' title the eighth time in a row. Wolff's rivalry with Christian Horner, owner and team principal of Red Bull Racing, is a cornerstone of the drama of the current F1 scene. Red Bull won four consecutive Constructors' titles from 2010 to 2013, with Sebastian Vettel winning the Drivers' title on each occasion. But in 2021, Red Bull finished 28 points adrift of Mercedes in the Constructors' Championship, further extending Wolff's winning run.

» Wolff looks a happy man during Mercedes' absolutely dominant 2015 season

04 ROSS BRAWN
HONDA (2008), BRAWN (2009), MERCEDES (2010–2013)

Ross Brawn only has a single Constructors' title to his credit, the 2009 championship, which was won with a car bearing his name and driven by Jenson Button, who took the Drivers' title the same year. Nevertheless, Brawn deserves his place in the top five team principals due to his influence on the sport in which he held vital roles in teams that have won eight Constructors' Championships and eight Drivers' Championships. As it was to transpire, Brawn GP only competed in the 2009 F1 World Championship, in the hiatus between the withdrawal of Honda from the sport and their takeover and rebranding as Mercedes GP from 2010. Brawn remained as team principal at Mercedes for three further seasons, but left at the end of 2013 – just before Mercedes began a run of unprecedented dominance. The rumour was that Brawn and Mercedes couldn't agree on his role, with Brawn wanting to remain in charge. Although Ross Brawn announced his retirement from the sport in 2014, at the start of 2017 he was appointed managing director, motorsports and technical director for the Formula 1 Group, where he continues to be heavily involved in the sport.

» Brawn on the starting grid at the 2009 German Grand Prix

03 RON DENNIS
MCLAREN (1980–2009, 2014–2016)

Ron Dennis was team principal at McLaren for an incredible 29 years, from 1980 to 2009. Even then he wasn't quite done with the team, returning as principal for a further two years between 2014 and 2016, before finally calling it a day. In the early years, Dennis had legendary chassis designer John Barnard on the team, who was responsible for first coming up with the concept of carbon-fibre chassis rather than aluminium alloy ones. Blessed with some of the all-time greats driving for his team, including Niki Lauda, Alain Prost and Ayrton Senna, Dennis racked up seven Constructors' Championships and ten Drivers' Championships. Obsessive, driven and ruthlessly single-minded, Dennis was a team principal in every sense of the term: there was never any doubt that he was in total charge. Dennis's success was most probably down to the fact that he could combine blue-sky thinking about the direction of travel for his next car with an attention to detail that was second to none. He also gained a reputation for a cautious and complex style of speaking, which was born out of a desire to remain in control through the ups and downs of life in the most volatile of sports.

« Dennis looks thoughtful during practice for the 2016 Bahrain Grand Prix

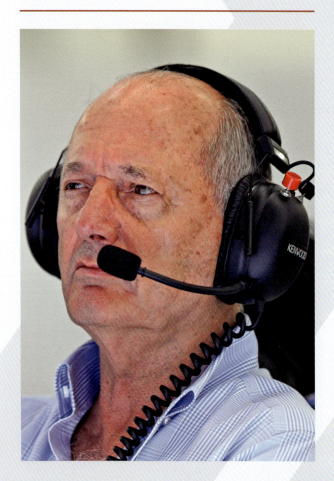

02 COLIN CHAPMAN
LOTUS (1958–1982)

Colin Chapman was the founder and driving force behind Lotus. Not just Team Lotus, the company's F1 arm, but Lotus Cars itself. An engineer by training, Chapman formed a strong partnership with the great Jim Clark: together they won the 1963 and 1965 F1 titles for both driver and constructor, and in 1965 they added the Indy 500 title for good measure. Clark should have won the 1964 title too, but a lack of reliability in the second half of the season cost him dear. Clark's death in 1968 hit Chapman hard, but he recovered and went on to claim further Constructors' titles in 1968, 1970, 1972, 1973 and 1978. Chapman's later years were overshadowed by his involvement in the John DeLorean scandal that defrauded the British taxpayer. However, this should not detract from his legacy to F1, which can be seen in his introduction of struts as a rear suspension device (still called Chapman struts); a monocoque chassis that was lighter and stronger than its predecessor, giving the driver more protection; the use of 'wings' to increase positive downforce; and the repositioning of the radiator from the front of the car to the sides to reduce aerodynamic drag.

⌃ Chapman at the 1970 Italian Grand Prix

⟩⟩ Williams at the launch of the 2006 Williams F1 car

01 FRANK WILLIAMS
WILLIAMS (1977–2020)

It's hard to know where to start with Frank Williams. It's not just the nine Constructors' titles that define him, or the seven different drivers who have won the Drivers' title while employed by Williams. Nor is it solely down to the fact that Williams had to overcome more obstacles than anyone to reach the pinnacle of his chosen career. Williams had no background in motorsport, no source of funds to make initial inroads and no connections he could use to get a start in a business that had always fascinated him. It was meeting designer Patrick Head in the late 1960s which was to prove a seminal moment for both men. In 1977 he and Head became partners and established Williams Grand Prix Engineering, initially run from a converted carpet warehouse in Didcot, England. Between 1980 and 1997, Williams won nine Constructors' titles. Nothing slowed them down – not the departure of world champions Nigel Mansell, Alain Prost and Damon Hill from the team when negotiations over a new contract broke down; nor Ayrton Senna's fatal crash at San Marino; not even Williams' own terrible accident in 1986.

In March of that year he was driving a rental car from the Paul Ricard Circuit to Nice airport for a flight home when he crashed. The accident left Williams near death on more than one occasion, and with the certainty of being a tetraplegic should he survive. Incredibly, 12 weeks later he was back home and less than a week after that he turned up at the factory in Didcot. His survival was down to a combination of iron will and a high level of personal fitness, which was thanks to a lifelong love of running. But Williams was not content with mere survival. He was determined to get back to doing what he did best – and loved the most – racing cars. Among his many attributes (Williams was an accomplished linguist) were an ability to solve problems and a laser-like focus, and he brought those to bear on his personal circumstances as he did his management of a racing team. At the time of his accident, Williams' family were told his life expectancy was unlikely to be ten years. That he not only lived for 36 years but won seven Constructors' titles in the process tells you everything about this remarkable man.